THE WICCAN BOOK OF SHADOWS

THE WICCAN BOOK OF SHADOWS

A MAGICAL GUIDE TO PERSONALIZING YOUR OWN SPELLS AND RITUALS

AMBROSIA HAWTHORN

ILLUSTRATIONS BY STUDIO MUTI

ROCKRIDGE
PRESS

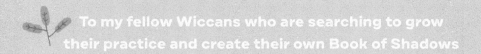
To my fellow Wiccans who are searching to grow their practice and create their own Book of Shadows

For general information on our other products and services or to obtain technical support, please contact our Customer Care Department within the United States at (866) 744-2665, or outside the United States at (510) 253-0500.

Rockridge Press publishes its books in a variety of electronic and print formats. Some content that appears in print may not be available in electronic books, and vice versa.

TRADEMARKS: Rockridge Press and the Rockridge Press logo are trademarks or registered trademarks of Callisto Media Inc. and/or its affiliates, in the United States and other countries, and may not be used without written permission. All other trademarks are the property of their respective owners. Rockridge Press is not associated with any product or vendor mentioned in this book.

Interior and Cover Designer: Erik Jacobsen
Art Producer: Samantha Ulban
Editor: Kelly Koester
Production Manager: Giraud Lorber
Production Editor: Sigi Nacson
Illustrations © 2020 Studio Muti

ISBN: Print 978-1-64739-929-0 | Ebook 978-1-64739-930-6
R0

THE WICCAN BOOK OF SHADOWS

A MAGICAL GUIDE TO PERSONALIZING YOUR OWN SPELLS AND RITUALS

AMBROSIA HAWTHORN

ILLUSTRATIONS BY STUDIO MUTI

ROCKRIDGE
PRESS

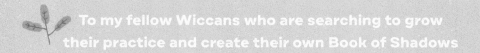

To my fellow Wiccans who are searching to grow their practice and create their own Book of Shadows

Interior and Cover Designer: Erik Jacobsen
Art Producer: Samantha Ulban
Editor: Kelly Koester
Production Manager: Giraud Lorber
Production Editor: Sigi Nacson
Illustrations © 2020 Studio Muti

ISBN: Print 978-1-64739-929-0 | Ebook 978-1-64739-930-6
R0

This Book of Shadows belongs to:

_____

Contents

Introduction

Merry meet and welcome to *The Wiccan Book of Shadows*, your guide to developing your own unique magical practice. "Merry meet" is a common Wiccan greeting, akin to saying, "Hello, it's nice to meet you." Wicca, often called the religion of witchcraft, is a fast-growing, Earth-centered belief system rooted in respect for nature and a reverence for the divine. It's based on pre-Christian traditions found in northern and western Europe, and has been practiced widely since the 1950s, when Gerald Gardner, the "father of Wicca," wrote several popular books on the subject. Wicca doesn't have a strict set of rules, beliefs, or practices that everyone follows. Each practitioner develops their own values and ethics, and sets their own rules. We all find Wicca for our own reasons that are unique to us.

Because Wicca has no singular set of rules, maintaining a record of your own beliefs and practices is very important to most practitioners. That's why many Wiccans today maintain a Book of Shadows, a volume that is home for their spells, rituals, recipes, and any other information important to their path. Having a Book of Shadows not only assists with the growth of your practice, it also provides a chance to discover and grow your knowledge. This sacred tool houses the core elements of the Wiccan path, and it can be as personalized as you'd like. There's no right or wrong way to make a Book of Shadows.

This book will offer you a space to personalize, reflect on, and develop your own magical practice. The first part of the book contains an in-depth study of Wiccan history, beliefs, and traditions, while the second part presents spells, rituals, and recipes with templates included for you to make your own. You'll also find write-in lines throughout for you to personalize and take notes for your own Book of Shadows. This book is intended to be accessible to practitioners at all levels, but it doesn't exhaustively cover every single element that a beginner needs to learn. If you're in that camp, I suggest potentially pairing this book with my other book, *Seasons of Wicca*.

Wicca has been an important part of my life since I was a teenager. I began my journey similarly to most, seeking a path of judgment-free faith and the ability to create positive changes for myself. I wasn't satisfied with traditional religions and their structured ways. Today, I'm both a practicing Wiccan and witch, with 16 years dedicated to my eclectic practice. I'm also the editor of *Witchology Magazine*, a monthly publication for modern witches, as well as the author of *The Spell Book for New Witches* and the aforementioned *Seasons of Wicca*.

My own Book of Shadows is a leather journal that was gifted to me by my partner. It contains correspondences for herbs, crystals, and deities, as well as recipes, rituals for the eight pagan Sabbats (or sun celebrations) and the 12 full moon Esbats, and the rules I live by.

Perhaps you've been practicing for as long as you can remember. Or maybe you've just recently stumbled upon the wonderful world of Wicca. Wherever you are on your journey, you picked up this book at the right time. I wish you well on your journey and hope that the ideas, lessons, and philosophies contained in this book benefit you. Let's dive into the enchanting world of Wicca beliefs and practices.

Merry part and merry meet again,
Ambrosia Hawthorn

PART I

THE ENCHANTING HISTORY, BELIEFS, AND TRADITIONS OF WICCA

Before we start building your Book of Shadows, let's delve into the traditions of Wicca. Starting with the basics of Wiccan history and beliefs, and moving on to the major holidays, traditions, and symbols, we'll get a solid overview of how these practices developed and how they're put into action today. These foundations are important to learn; they'll help you establish a firm base to grow from and connect you to Wicca's history.

CHAPTER **1**

Wiccan History and Beliefs

Wicca is very diverse and inviting to those who seek a path centered around nature and the divine. With Wicca, there is no governing body, and there are no renowned prophets. Instead, there are many decisions that you get to make as a Wiccan regarding the laws, beliefs, and traditions you engage with and honor. These decisions are important foundations for a successful and long-lasting practice. To make these decisions properly, it's important to understand each tradition's purpose and history.

The Wiccan Rede

The Wiccan Rede is the moral system of Wicca. It is not a command-ment or law, but it *is* a guideline. The word *rede* derives from Middle English, meaning "advice" or "counsel," which is a principle to avoid causing harm. Gerald Gardner (1884–1964), in his groundbreaking 1957 Wiccan book, *The Meaning of Witchcraft*, introduces his set of laws or "Ardanes," which includes: "You must not use magic for anything which will cause harm to anyone, and if, to prevent a greater wrong being done, you must discommode someone, you must do it only in a way which will abate the harm."

The most famous version of the Rede is Doreen Valiente (1922–1999)'s 1964 couplet: "An' ye harm none, do what ye will." "An" is an archaic word meaning "if."

The second most popular mention of the Rede is in a 1975 poem titled *The Rede of the Wiccae* by Lady Gwen Thompson (1928–1986), published in the American pagan magazine *Green Egg*.

Lady Gwen is known for the long version of the Wiccan Rede and credited her grandmother, Adriana Porter, with the original work. Although there is no scholarly evidence for this claim, this Rede remains one of the most popular writings in Wicca today. Here's an excerpt of Lady Gwen's Rede:

Eight words ye Wiccan Rede fulfill:

An' it harm none, do what ye will.

Prior to Gerald Gardner, Aleister Crowley (1875–1947), creator of the religion Thelema, mentions, "Do what thou wilt shall be the whole of the Law" (verse I:40) in his 1904 *The Book of the Law*.

All these references contain a similar message, which is universal to all Wiccan Redes today: Harm none. It's the pillar of what Wicca stands for—respecting others, being free, and having no judgment. However, each practitioner will either follow the Rede or construct a personal code of ethics in their practice that suits them. While not all Wiccans include the Wiccan Rede in their Book of Shadows, many do.

Does the Wiccan Rede resonate with you? Which version best connects with your personal beliefs?

_____

_____

_____

_____

_____

The History of Wicca

Wicca is a deeply nuanced and ever-evolving religion, and its history begins with the teachings of Gerald Gardner. Wicca was created as a way to honor and spread the witch-cult teachings of Margaret Murray, the Thelema philosophy of Aleister Crowley, and the Italian traditions of folk witchcraft collected by Charles Leland. All these works had a theme of reviving ancient pagan beliefs and religions.

Gardner, who was a member of England's New Forest coven in the late 1930s, compiled notes about these various traditions before founding the Gardnerian Wicca tradition, the first of its kind, in the 1940s. Gardner was the first person to use the term _Wicca_ (though he spelled it "Wica") to refer to a tradition of witchcraft—he wrote about it in his 1954 book, _Witchcraft Today_. In the 1950s, Doreen Valiente was initiated and became the Gardnerian Wicca tradition's High Priestess. She was instrumental in adapting the written work of the coven.

Wicca falls under the umbrella of paganism, but is technically considered a form of neo-paganism. While paganism encompasses the historical religions of the past, neo-paganism refers to modern religions inspired by those past traditions. Although each neo-pagan path is different, many share the same ethic of doing no harm and embrace religious freedom, a reverence for nature, equality of the sexes, and openness to all forms of sexuality. Though Wicca began as a way to revive ancient traditions, it has evolved into a way for people to embrace their spirituality without the restrictions and dogma of organized religions. At the core of Wicca, anyone is accepted and welcomed, regardless of race, color, sex, age, national or cultural origins, or sexual preference.

It's important to note that while Wiccans and witches are pagans, not all witches are Wiccans, and not all Wiccans are witches. Witches may or may not choose to follow a religious path, and Wiccans may or may not practice magic.

While not all Wiccans practice magic, it's an integral part of manifestation and growth. *Magic* is defined as transformation or change for an intended purpose. Energy can be harnessed, transferred, manipulated, and charged according to your desires and intentions. When performing spells, rituals, and recipes with a purpose, you're creating magic.

What first drew you to Wicca? How has your relationship with it evolved and changed? Write about your own personal Wicca history.

Old Wicca versus Modern Wicca

Old Wicca (sometimes called "the old ways") refers to the traditions and practices set by Gerald Gardner, as well as those set by Alex Sanders (1926–1988), who brought the Gardnerian tradition to the United States in the 1960s. Back then, the terms *Wicca* and *witchcraft* were considered synonymous, which isn't the case today.

In the past, the only way to become Wiccan or learn about the craft was through rigorous training and initiation into one of the traditions, such as Gardnerian, Alexandrian, Dianic, Saxon, Celtic, or other Church of Wicca movements. Old Wicca was considered secretive and selective of its members. Many covens were created by former coven initiates; to become a High Priest or Priestess, you had to be a part of the coven for many years, studying and learning everything you could.

The works of Scott Cunningham (1956–1993) were the turning point in providing accessible information to the public about Wicca. Cunningham wrote more than 50 books, several of which were about magic, Wicca, and solo magical practice. Cunningham's books provided a new way of practicing Wicca that didn't require a coven initiation. In the past, if you wanted to find information on Wicca, you had to learn from the teachings of coven members as an initiate. But Cunningham believed that there shouldn't be secrets besides the ones a practitioner kept in their own practice. Cunningham tried being part of covens but opted for a solo practice, and wanted to share his knowledge with anyone who had an interest. This accessibility helped Wicca evolve into Neo-Wicca, which much of the practice consists of today.

Modern Wicca includes newer Wiccan traditions inspired by Old Wicca. Many practices of Old Wicca are still present in Modern Wicca, including incorporating the masculine and feminine aspects of divinity and performing rituals for holidays, phases of the moon, equinoxes and solstices, the elements, initiations, and other important life phases.

Wicca changes and adapts with the times, but its core values and beliefs remain the same—honoring nature, the seasons or Sabbats, and divinity, and practicing ethics. Modern Wicca is eclectic in nature, meaning that it derives from different ideas and diverse sources. Wicca today is considered amorphous and can easily have roots in various beliefs or practices. My practice, for example, consists of Wicca and witchcraft that encompass astrology, tarot, herbalism, and spirit work. All you have to do is follow your heart to the path that's right for you.

What do you do in your own practice? What inspires your traditions?

_____

_____

_____

_____

_____

Blessed Beliefs

The blessed beliefs of Wiccan practice consist of working with nature, deity, ethics, and harmony. Each can be custom-tailored to your practice, so that it better aligns with your own beliefs.

Nature: As an Earth-centered religion, Wicca respects all kinds of life and cares for the environment. When it comes to your own practice, what does that look like? Do you make the decision to use reusables? Reduce your carbon footprint? Plant gardens or trees? Hold rituals for the elements?

Ethics and Harmony: Throughout Wicca, we see the importance of ethics and making sure to "harm none." Another important part of Wicca is free will. Just as you get to decide what path you will take, others should be able to make their own choices, free from manipulation. In balance and harmony, if you take, you should give. Do you follow the Wiccan Rede or your own ethics?

When working with magic, rituals, or spells, take the time to create a code of ethics outlining boundaries you'd like to make for your practice. You are free to do as you choose, but you are also responsible for your actions.

Deity: When it comes to working with deity, you again have options. Within Wicca, animist, deist, theist, or atheist beliefs can be put into practice. There's no one prescribed way to practice or single being you must believe in. Through trial and error, find what works for you.

→ **Animism** is the belief that objects, places, and creatures all possess a distinct spiritual essence. These beliefs are often found in indigenous practices and shamanism.

→ **Deism** is the belief in supreme beings or a creator who does not intervene in the universe. Deism rejects supernatural aspects of religion, such as rituals or events. (The words *deism* and *theism* are both derived from words meaning "god" and were considered synonymous until the 17th century.)

→ **Theism** is the belief in deity. It's often divided into the subcategories of pantheism, panentheism, polytheism, duotheism, and monotheism.

→ **Pantheism** is the belief that the natural world and God are the same, as "pan" means "all" and "theism" means "God." It represents God as "all-encompassing" and regards the universe as a manifestation of God. This is seen in the common Wiccan practice of honoring the Lord and Lady or God and Goddess, who are supreme deities. In pantheism, Wiccan deities are often also referred to as the Horned God and the Triple Goddess.

→ **Panentheism** is the belief that deity is in everything, and that the deity is greater than the universe. The addition of "en" in panentheism, meaning "in," makes it different from pantheism.

→ **Polytheism** is a belief in multiple gods and goddesses, including many different deities taken from various pagan pantheons. This allows for a multitude of different pantheons and religions to be included.

→ **Duotheism** is the belief in two equal deities, such as the God and Goddess. This is seen throughout Wicca as belief in the Lord and Lady or God and Goddess, and is often paired with pantheism, panentheism, and polytheism.

→ **Monotheism** is the belief in one God or Goddess. This is seen in Dianic Wiccans, who often only believe in the Goddess aspect of divinity, or Christian witches, who practice witchcraft within a Christian framework and honor Jesus and Mary as God and Goddess together. Though there's been controversy within the magical community about Christian witches, at Wicca's core, there is no judgment for self-identifying as one path over another.

→ **Atheism** is the absence of belief in the existence of deities, which contrasts with theism. This is often seen in secular witches.

How do you self-identify?

The 13 Principles of the Council of American Witches

Although Wicca doesn't have laws or rules, a set of principles was created in 1973 by practitioners from a variety of magical backgrounds and traditions who called themselves the Council of American Witches. These principles were an attempt to unify the various paths of the pagan community. These principles are:

1. We practice rites to attune ourselves with the natural rhythm of life forces marked by the phases of the moon and the seasonal quarters and cross-quarters.

2. We recognize that our intelligence gives us a unique responsibility toward our environment. We seek to live in harmony with nature, in ecological balance offering fulfillment to life and consciousness within an evolutionary concept.

3. We acknowledge a depth of power far greater than what is apparent to the average person. Because it is far greater than ordinary, it is sometimes called "supernatural," but we see it as lying within that which is naturally potential to all.

4. We conceive of the Creative Power in the universe as manifesting through polarity—as masculine and feminine—and that this same Creative Power lies in all people, and functions through the interaction of the masculine and feminine. We value neither above the other, knowing each to be supportive of the other. We value sex as pleasure, as the symbol and embodiment of life, and as one of the sources of energies used in magickal practice and religious worship.

5. We recognize both outer and inner, or psychological, worlds— sometimes known as the Spiritual World, the Collective Unconscious, Inner Planes, etc.—and we see in the interaction of

these two dimensions the basis for paranormal phenomena and magickal exercises. We neglect neither dimension for the other, seeing both as necessary for our fulfillment.

6. We do not recognize any authoritarian hierarchy but do honor those who teach, respect those who share their greater knowledge and wisdom, and acknowledge those who have courageously given of themselves in leadership.

7. We see religion, magick, and wisdom-in-living as being united in the way one views the world and lives within it—a worldview and philosophy of life which we identify as Witchcraft, the Wiccan Way.

8. Calling oneself "Witch" does not make one a Witch—but neither does heredity itself, nor the collecting of titles, degrees, and initiations. A Witch seeks to control the forces within her/himself that make life possible in order to live wisely and well, without harm to others and in harmony with nature.

9. We believe in the affirmation and fulfillment of life in a continuation of evolution and development of consciousness that gives meaning to the universe we know, and our personal role within it.

10. Our only animosity toward Christianity, or toward any other religion or philosophy of life, is to the extent that its institutions have claimed to be "the only way" and have sought to deny freedom to others and to suppress other ways of religious practice and belief.

11. As American Witches, we are not threatened by debates on the history of the Craft, the origins of various terms, or the origins of various aspects of different traditions. We are concerned with our present and our future.

12. We do not accept the concept of absolute evil, nor do we worship any entity known as Satan or the Devil, as defined by Christian tradition. We do not seek power through the suffering

of others, nor do we accept that personal benefit can be derived only by denial to another.

13. We believe that we should seek within nature that which is contributory to our health and well-being.

While The Council of American Witches disbanded after a year, it is still my hope that you'll see the beauty of Wicca and how it enables you to create your own traditions, practices, and beliefs. These principles are not strict rules but only guidance and advice.

Do any of these principles resonate with you? If so, which ones and why? If not, what beliefs do? Write about your Wiccan principles.

_____

_____

_____

_____

_____

Wicca and the Natural World

A profound respect for nature and a connection with the natural world are the foundations of Wicca. The natural world is home to the planet's movements, cycles, and rhythms of growth, harvest, decay, and regeneration. Wiccans also feel a connection to divinity through the Earth.

In working with the natural world, Wiccans incorporate the five elements, the four seasons, the solstices, the equinoxes, the twelve (or thirteen) full moons each year, and the eight pagan Sabbats: Samhain, Yule, Imbolc, Ostara, Beltane, Litha, Lughnasadh, and Mabon.

You can use natural items in your practice to connect with ancient wisdom and the divine in nature. Try crystals, herbs, wooden items, feathers, bones, and minerals. With these items, you can craft and create recipes, spells, rituals, and offerings all imbued with natural intention and energy.

The Five Elements

The five elements of air, fire, water, earth, and spirit allow Wiccans to work with the natural world. The elements also connect with specific astrological signs, tarot arcana, cardinal directions, seasons, and deities.

Air

→ **Goddesses:** Arianrhod (Celtic), Aura (Greek/Roman), Cardea (Greek/Roman), Nuit (Egyptian)

→ **Gods:** Amun (Egyptian), Shu (Egyptian), Borrum (Celtic), Odin (Norse)

→ **Tarot:** Suit of Swords, Fool, Magician, Lovers, Justice, Star

→ **Ritual tools:** Feather, athame, incense

→ **Season:** Spring

→ **Gender:** Masculine

→ **Color:** Yellow

→ **Qualities:** Communication, psychic powers, inspiration, imagination, ideas, knowledge, wishes, the mind

→ **Cardinal direction:** East

→ **Pentacle placement:** Upper left

→ **Stones:** Topaz, pumice, rainbow stones, crystals, amethyst, alexandrite

→ **Zodiac signs:** Gemini, Libra, Aquarius

Fire

→ **Goddesses:** Brighid (Celtic), Sekhmet (Egyptian), Hestia/Vesta (Greek/Roman)
→ **Gods:** Aed (Celtic), Horus (Egyptian), Prometheus (Greek/ Roman), Hephaestus/Vulcan (Greek/Roman), Ra (Egyptian)
→ **Ritual tools:** Wand, candles
→ **Tarot:** Suit of Wands, Emperor, Strength, Wheel of Fortune, Temperance, Tower, Sun, Judgement
→ **Season:** Summer
→ **Gender:** Masculine
→ **Color:** Red
→ **Qualities:** Energy, inspiration, love, passion, leadership
→ **Cardinal direction:** South
→ **Pentacle placement:** Lower right
→ **Stones:** Ruby, fire opal, volcanic lava, agate
→ **Zodiac signs:** Aries, Leo, Sagittarius

Water

→ **Goddesses:** Venus/Aphrodite (Roman/Greek), Anuket (Egypt), Boann (Celtic), Isis (Egyptian), Styx (Greek), Coventina (Celtic)
→ **Gods:** Neptune/Poseidon (Roman/Greek), Lir (Celtic)
→ **Tarot:** Suit of Cups, High Priestess, Chariot, Hanged Man, Death, Moon
→ **Ritual tools:** Chalice, cauldron
→ **Season:** Autumn
→ **Gender:** Feminine
→ **Color:** Blue
→ **Qualities:** Emotion, absorption, subconscious, purification, eternal movement, wisdom, the soul
→ **Cardinal direction:** West
→ **Pentacle placement:** Upper right
→ **Stones:** Aquamarine, amethyst, blue tourmaline, pearl, coral, blue topaz, fluorite
→ **Zodiac signs:** Cancer, Scorpio, Pisces

Earth

→ **Goddesses:** Demeter/Ceres (Greek/Roman), Gaia/Terra (Greek/Roman), Persephone/Proserpina (Greek/Roman), Cybele/Magna Mater (Greek/Roman), Rhea/Ops (Greek/ Roman), Freyja (Norse), Joro (Norse), Sif (Norse)

→ **Gods:** Apollo (Greek/Roman), Cernunnos (Celtic), Dionysus/Bacchus (Greek/Roman), Geb (Egyptian), Pan/Faunus (Greek/Roman), Ullr (Norse)

→ **Tarot:** Suit of Pentacles, Empress, Hierophant, Hermit, Devil, World

→ **Ritual tools:** Pentacle, salt, crystals

→ **Season:** Winter

→ **Gender:** Feminine

→ **Spirits:** Gnomes, dwarfs, trolls

→ **Color:** Green

→ **Qualities:** Abundance, femininity, prosperity, grounding, stability, strength, wealth

→ **Cardinal direction:** North

→ **Pentacle placement:** Lower left

→ **Stones:** Emerald, onyx, jasper, salt, azurite, amethyst, quartz

→ **Zodiac signs:** Capricorn, Taurus, Virgo

Spirit (or Aether)

→ **Deities:** God and Goddess (Wicca)

→ **Season:** Wheel of the Year

→ **Gender:** Universal

→ **Cycle of life:** Eternity

→ **Color:** White

→ **Energy:** Universal

→ **Qualities:** Connection, balance, presence in all things

→ **Cardinal direction:** Central

→ **Pentacle placement:** Top

→ **Stones:** Any

→ **Zodiac signs:** Any

Moon Magic and Lore

In addition to working with the natural world, seasons, and cycles, Wiccans celebrate and observe the monthly moon phases: new moon, waxing crescent, first quarter, waxing gibbous, full moon, waning gibbous, last quarter, and waning crescent. The moon is celebrated during Esbats and honors the Goddess and her aspects of Maiden, Mother, and Crone. Each moon cycle lasts 29.5 days, which is a little longer than the 27.3 days that the moon takes to orbit the Earth. Each phase of the moon holds unique energy and power, and knowing how to harness that energy is beneficial to your practice.

For an easy reference, waxing *means growing energy, and* waning *means fading energy.*

New Moon: The beginning of the lunar cycle, when the moon is fully cast in shadow and invisible to the naked eye. This moon offers limitless potential and new beginnings, so it's a great time to plant the seeds of new ideas. This is also a perfect time for working with the energy of personal improvement, manifestation, and divination.

Waxing Crescent: In this phase, the moon looks like a sliver in the sky, symbolizing the Maiden aspect of the Goddess. It's a time to explore your dreams and growth and is ideal for working with the energy of action, courage, faith, love, and abundance.

First Quarter: This moon marks the halfway point between a new moon and a full moon. During this phase, as the moon's strength is growing, it's an excellent time to work with the energy of creativity, luck, courage, healing, finances, balance, motivation, and love.

Waxing Gibbous: The phase just before the full moon. This moon's energy reflects stamina, progress, adjustment, success, finances, patience, and nurturing, as well as progress and staying on course.

Full Moon: This phase, when the moon is fully illuminated in the sky, is the Mother aspect of the Goddess. The moon's energy is strongest during this time and is often used to charge tools. The full moon phase is perfect for energy relating to spirituality, results, decisions, gratitude, forgiveness, healing, and success. Some Wiccans perform an Esbat, or a full moon ritual, during this time.

Waning Gibbous: This phase, when the moon begins its descent toward the end of the cycle, is a good time for working with energy relating to grounding, release, relaxation, regrouping, acceptance, elimination, banishing, transitions, obstacles, and balance.

Last Quarter: This moon marks the halfway point between a full moon and new moon. During this phase, the moon's energy continues to lessen and is ideal for adjustment, relaxation, acceptance, regrouping, turning inward, meditation, and lower energy work.

Waning Crescent: This phase, when the moon becomes a sliver in the sky, just before the new moon, is the Crone aspect of the Goddess. It's a time for rest, intuition, banishing, protection, cleansing, meditation, and lower energy work.

The Power of the Sun

The Sun has equal power to the moon and represents the God during the solstices, equinoxes, and cross-quarter days. Together, these solar days and halfway celebrations make up the eight pagan Sabbats: Samhain, Yule, Imbolc, Ostara, Beltane, Litha, Lughnasadh, and Mabon. Each Sabbat is a celebration honoring the changing of seasons and energy of the Earth. Sabbat comes from the Latin word *sabbatum*, meaning "day of rest." You can harness the solar energy of the God during these sun celebrations, or Sabbats.

Celestial Power

The Sun and Moon, our celestial neighbors, hold great power in Wicca, so it makes sense that the rest of the planets and stars would have significance, as well. In your practice, you can choose to work with the planets Mercury, Venus, Mars, Jupiter, Saturn, Neptune, Uranus, and Pluto. Yes, even though Pluto has been downgraded to a dwarf planet, it is still very much used in Wiccan practice, as its energy is still felt.

To work with the planets, you can tap into their energy, delve into astrology and birth charts, or work with the deities associated with each planet. There are also four asteroids—the first ever discovered— that are also referred to as the "asteroid goddesses": Pallas Athena, Vesta, Juno, and Ceres.

Planets and Deities

Sun

Deities: Horned God (Wicca), Helios/Sol (Greek/Roman), Apollo (Greek/Roman), Ra (Egypt), Lugh (Celtic), Sól (Norse)

Qualities: The ego, sense of purpose, vitality

Meaning: God of Prophecy and Solar Incarnation

Moon

Deities: Triple Goddess (Wicca), Artemis/Diana (Greek/Roman), Selene/Luna (Greek/Roman), Hecate (Greek)

Qualities: Emotions, motherly instincts

Meaning: Goddess of Earth, Hunting, and Lunar Incarnation

Mercury

Deities: Hermes/Mercury (Greek/ Roman)

Qualities: Communication, mind, intelligence

Meaning: God of Messengers and Travel

Venus

Deities: Aphrodite/Venus (Greek/ Roman)

Qualities: Fertility, beauty, and enthusiasm

Meaning: Goddess of Romance and Lust

Mars

Deities: Ares/Mars (Greek/ Roman)

Qualities: Strength, action

Meaning: God of War

Jupiter

Deities: Zeus/Jupiter (Greek/ Roman)

Qualities: Teacher, luck, expansion

Meaning: Leader of the Olympian Gods

Saturn

Deities: Cronus/Saturn (Greek/ Roman)

Qualities: Ambition, status, duty, wisdom, patience, honor, authority, hardship

Meaning: God of Agriculture

Uranus

Deities: Ouranos/Caelus (Greek/ Roman)

Qualities: Originality, eccentricity, change

Meaning: Incarnation of the Sky

Neptune

Deities: Poseidon/Neptune (Greek/Roman)

Qualities: Dreams, illusions, psychic receptivity

Meaning: God of the Sea

Pluto

Deities: Hades/Pluto (Greek/ Roman)

Qualities: Rebirth, subconscious forces

Meaning: God of the Underworld

Asteroid Goddesses

Ceres

Deities: Demeter/Ceres (Greek/Roman)

Qualities: Power, strength, might, energy, self-worth

Meaning: Goddess of the Harvest and Seasons

Pallas Athena

Deities: Pallas Athena/Minerva (Greek/Roman)

Qualities: Wisdom, artistry, justice, strength, courage

Meaning: Virgin Goddess of Wisdom, Fertility, and Arts

Vesta

Deities: Hestia/Vesta (Greek/Roman)

Qualities: Domestic life, home, commitment, inner strength

Meaning: Virgin Goddess of the Hearth and Home

Juno

Deities: Juno/Hera (Greek/Roman)

Qualities: Women's lives, principles, jealousy, equality

Meaning: Goddess of Marriage and Childbirth

Wiccan Deities

Wiccan belief is often centered around a duotheistic path, meaning belief in the existence of two deities—the God and Goddess. Together, they complement each other, while also being opposing forces of roughly equal power. This is similar to the concept of yin and yang, where yin represents femininity, and yang, masculinity. The God is represented by the Sun, while the Goddess is represented by the moon. The Goddess is personified during the four earth festivals of Imbolc, Beltane, Lammas, and Samhain. Other deities include the pantheons of Celtic, Norse, Egyptian, Greek, and Roman gods.

But while working with the God and Goddess may be common, there is no prescribed way to practice, no one being to believe in. It's a decision you make for yourself.

The Goddess

For Wiccans, the Goddess is the all-encompassing feminine counterpart to the God. She is called the Lady, Mother Goddess, or Triple Goddess because she has three forms or aspects: Maiden, Mother, and Crone.

Maiden: The youthful phase of a woman's life

Qualities: Innocence, youth, enchantment, discovery, independence, creativity, the promise of new beginnings

Season: Spring

Time of day: Dawn/morning

Sabbats: Imbolc, Ostara

Goddesses: Artemis/Diana (Greek/Roman), Persephone/Proserpina (Greek/Roman), Freyja (Norse), Rhiannon (Celtic), Hathor (Egyptian)

Mother: A time of maturity, motherhood

Qualities: Fertility, sexuality, adulthood, responsibility, stability, power

Season: Summer

Time of day: Midday

Sabbats: Beltane, Litha, Lughnasadh

Goddesses: Demeter/Ceres (Greek/Roman), Danu (Celtic), Selene (Roman), Isis (Egyptian)

Crone: The post-childbearing years of life or "hag" phase

Qualities: Wisdom, compassion, prophecy, death, aging, endings

Seasons: Autumn, winter

Time of day: Dusk/night

Sabbats: Mabon, Samhain, and Yule

Goddesses: Hecate/Hekate (Greek/Roman), Morrighan (Celtic), Cailleach (Celtic)

In some neo-pagan circles, the Maiden, the Mother, and the Crone are worshipped alongside a fourth, known as the Queen, the Enchantress, or Wise Woman. This fourth face represents those who have grown out of the Mother phase but are not yet in the Crone phase, or those who go a different direction from motherhood. This face of the Goddess relates to the Autumn season and the waning energies of summer and life. If you choose to honor this aspect, the above list will be altered to have a few qualities of both the Mother and the Crone. If you look at the seasons, elements, tarot suits, and Moon phases, there are four aspects. So, for many, it's easy to see a fourth aspect of the Goddess, especially with the way society is ever evolving.

Queen/Enchantress/Wise Woman: Older and mature, but not a mother

Qualities: Power, stability, wisdom

Season: Autumn

Time of day: Dusk

Sabbats: Lughnasadh, Mabon

Goddesses: Medusa (Greek/Roman), Freyja (Norse), Demeter/Ceres (Greek/Roman)

The Goddess is vital to the Wiccan faith. Every one of her aspects is just as important as the last and depending on what phase of your life you're in, one form may call out to you more than the others. But no matter which phase seems most personally compelling, don't neglect the others because together, they constitute the full being of the Goddess in all of her divinity. It's important to also note that these phases don't solely reflect the fertility of a woman but the phases of life in general.

The Goddess is most often represented by the triple moon symbol—which is composed of a waxing crescent moon, full moon, and waning crescent moon—as well as by a triple spiral, a circle, and silver candle. Another popular symbol is the goddess spiral. Spirals, in general, represent journey, direction, and progress.

The God

The God is the all-encompassing masculine counterpart to the Goddess. He is called the Lord, Horned God, or Sun God. He is associated with nature, wilderness, sexuality, hunting, and cycles. Similar to the Goddess, the God has aspects such as Cernunnos, the Green Man, or the Oak and Holly Kings. The God is personified during the four solar festivals of Yule, Litha, Ostara, and Mabon. In other pantheons, the God is often seen as Pan/Faunus (Greek/Roman), Brân (Welsh), Herne (Celtic), Apollo (Greek/Roman), Osiris (Egyptian), and Janus (Roman).

The God is represented by horns or antlers, a gold candle, or phallic symbols such as a wand.

Other Wiccan Deities

There are thousands of different deities; the ones you choose to honor will often depend on what pantheon your spiritual path follows. If you're eclectic like me, you might even choose to draw from multiple pantheons, honoring a god of one tradition beside a goddess of another. There are some gods and goddesses commonly invoked in Wicca.

Greek/Roman Pantheon

Aphrodite/Venus (Goddess of Love)

Ares/Mars (God of War)

Artemis/Diana (Goddess of the Hunt and Motherhood)

Athena/Minerva (Goddess of War and Wisdom)

Chloris/Flora (Goddess of Flowers and Plants)

Demeter/Ceres (Goddess of the Harvest)

Eos/Aurora (Goddess of the Dawn)

Eros/Cupid (God of Passion and Lust)

Gaia/Terra (Goddess of the Earth)

Hades/Pluto (God of the Underworld)

Hecate/Hekate (Goddess of Magic)

Hera/Juno (Goddess of Marriage)

Hestia/Vesta (Goddess of Hearth and Home)

Nemesis/Invidia (Goddess of Revenge)

Priapus/Mutunus (God of Fertility and Lust)

Zeus/Jupiter (Ruler of the pantheon)

Egyptian Pantheon

Aker (God of the Earth and Horizon)

Amaunet (Creator Goddess of Air and Wind)

Amun (Creator God of Sun and Air)

Anubis (God/Goddess of Death and Embalming)

Anuket (Goddess of the Hunt)

Bast (Goddess of Protection and Fertility)

Geb (God of the Earth)

Hathor (Goddess of the Sky, Women, and Fertility)

Horus (God of the Sun and Sky)

Isis (Mother Goddess)

Ma'at (Goddess of Truth and Balance)

Nut (Goddess of the Sky and Heavens)

Osiris (God of Death and Resurrection)

Ra (God of the Sun)

Renpet (Goddess of Spring and Fertility)

Sekhmet (Goddess of War)

Set (God of Chaos and Strength)

Tefnut (Goddess of Water and Rain)

Thoth (God of Moon, Magic, and Wisdom)

Celtic Pantheon

Áine (Goddess of Summer, Wealth, and Sovereignty)

Anu (Goddess of the Earth)

Arianrhod (Goddess of the Moon and Stars)

Belenos (God of Fire and Light)

Blodeuwedd (Goddess of Spring)

Boann (Goddess of Fertility, Inspiration, and Poetry)

Brân (God of Health and Regeneration)

Brighid (Goddess of the Hearth)

Cailleach (Goddess of Winter)

Cernunnos (Horned God)

Cerridwen (Goddess of the Cauldron and Underworld)

Creiddylad (Goddess of Flowers and Love)

Dagda (God of Fertility and Knowledge)

Danu (Mother Goddess)

Epona/Rhiannon (Goddess of Mares and Foals)

Lugh (God of Skills and Crafts)

Morrighan (Goddess of War)

Rhiannon (Goddess of Wisdom, Beauty, and Fertility)

Norse Pantheon

Baldur (God of Light)

Freyja (Goddess of Abundance and Fertility)

Freyr (God of Fertility and Peace)

Frigga (Goddess of Marriage and Prophecy)

Heimdall (God of Light, and is the keeper of the Bifrost Bridge)

Hel (Goddess of the Underworld)

Loki (God of Mischief)

Mani (God of the Moon)

Njord (God of the Sea)

Norns (Goddesses of Fate and Destiny)

Odin (God of War and Wisdom)

Sága (Goddess of Poetry and History)

Skadi (Goddess of Winter)

Thor (God of Thunder)

Tyr (God of War)

Ullr (God of Hunting and Sports)

Which deities speak to you? Why are you drawn to them?

_____

_____

_____

_____

_____

_____

_____

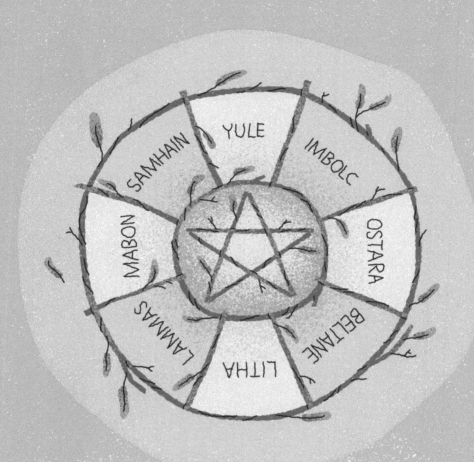

CHAPTER **2**

Wiccan Holidays, Traditions, and Sacred Symbolism

N ow that you know the basics of Wiccan history and beliefs, it's time to explore the major Wiccan holidays and traditions. We'll dive into the eight sun celebrations or pagan Sabbats and the twleve (often thirteen) full moons or Esbats, as well as the significance behind some powerful Wiccan symbols.

The Wiccan's Year

The Wiccan calendar is a little different from the Gregorian calendar that you use for your day-to-day life. The Wiccan year follows the Wheel of the Year, which is made up of the eight Sabbats (or sun celebrations) that mark the Earth's journey around the Sun. The Wiccan new year doesn't start on January 1; rather, it begins on Samhain, or the autumn equinox.

This isn't the only calendar a Wiccan might follow, either. An astrologer follows the astrological calendar; the astrological New Year is Ostara, or the spring equinox, which marks the date when the 12th zodiac sign of Aquarius moves into Aries, the first sign of the zodiac. Some Wiccans also follow the Celtic Tree Calendar, which has 13 moon divisions.

The Sabbats

There are eight Sabbats each year—four solar celebrations, known as the lesser Sabbats, and four Earth celebrations or cross-quarter days, also called the greater Sabbats. These celebrations follow the ebb and flow of nature and observe the changing seasons, and the terms *greater* and *lesser* refer to the corresponding energies of the Earth.

The four solar celebrations are the solstices, Yule and Litha, and the two equinoxes, Ostara and Mabon. The two solstices are often represented by two aspects of the Horned God: the Oak and Holly Kings. The Oak King hails from the light half of the year and represents the waxing or growing energy, while the Holly King is tied to the dark half of the year and represents the waning or dimming energy. At each solstice, there's a battle between the two kings; the Holly King wins during the summer solstice, or Litha, but the Oak King wins at the winter solstice, or Yule.

The four earth celebrations—Imbolc, Beltane, Lammas, and Samhain—mark the halfway points between the solar festivals. The Anglo-Saxons celebrated the solstices and equinoxes, while the Celts celebrated the fire festivals or cross-quarter days.

Yule (The Winter Solstice)

Also called: Winter Solstice, Midwinter, Witch's Christmas, or Yuletide

Celebrated: December 21–22 in the Northern Hemisphere and June 21–22 in the Southern Hemisphere

It honors the longest night of the year and the rebirth of the Sun or victory of the Oak King. Yule also represents the birth of the God.

Qualities: Death, rebirth, transformation, the darkness of night

Deities: The Crone (Wicca), Cailleach (Celtic), Demeter/Ceres (Greek/Roman), Frigga (Norse), Dionysus/Bacchus (Greek/Roman), Fauna/Bona Dea (Greek/Roman), Odin (Norse), Cronos/Saturn (Greek/Roman), Horned God (Wicca)

Imbolc

Also called: Candlemas, Imbolg, Brigid's Day, Lupercalia, or Oimelc

Celebrated: February 1 in the Northern Hemisphere and August 1 in the Southern Hemisphere

The first of the three spring festivals, Imbolc celebrates life's return to the Earth after winter. The Maiden Goddess is at full strength during this Sabbat.

Qualities: Fertility, love, creativity

Deities: The Maiden (Wicca), Aphrodite/Venus (Greek/Roman), Bast (Egyptian), Brighid (Celtic), Arianrhod (Celtic), Artemis/Diana (Greek/Roman), Athena/Minerva (Greek/Roman), Demeter/Ceres (Greek/Roman), Selene/Luna (Greek/Roman), Cerridwen (Celtic), Gaia/Terra

(Greek/Roman), Hestia/Vesta (Greek/Roman), Eros/Cupid (Greek/Roman), Pan/Faunus (Greek/Roman), Horned God (Wicca)

Ostara (The Spring Equinox)

Also called: Spring Equinox, Eostra's Day, or Vernal Equinox

Celebrated: March 20–21 in the Northern Hemisphere and September 20–21 in the Southern Hemisphere

During this Sabbat—the second of the three spring festivals—the hours of day and night will be equal. Ostara also represents the union between the God and Maiden Goddess.

Qualities: Renewal, balance, rebirth

Deities: The Maiden (Wicca), Eostre (Norse/Germanic), Freyja (Norse), Aphrodite/Venus (Greek/Roman), Herne (Celtic), Dagda (Celtic), Eros/Cupid (Greek/Roman), Osiris (Egyptian), Pan/Faunus (Greek/Roman), Green Man (Celtic), Thor (Norse), Horned God (Wicca)

Beltane

Also called: May Day or Beltain

Celebrated: May 1 in the Northern Hemisphere and November 1 in the Southern Hemisphere

During this Sabbat, the third spring festival, the veil between life and death is thin, just as it is on Samhain. Many use this time to work with spirits and fae. Beltane also represents the Mother Goddess at full power.

Qualities: New beginnings, passion, and romance

Deities: The Mother (Wicca), Eostre (Norse/Germanic), Freyja (Norse), Aphrodite/Venus (Greek/Roman), Blodeuwedd (Welsh), Eos/Aurora (Greek/Roman), Chloris/Flora (Greek/Roman), Gaia/Terra (Greek/Roman), Persephone/Proserpina (Greek/Roman), Renpet (Egypt), Apollo (Greek/Roman), Cernunnos (Celtic), Odin (Norse), Pan/Faunus

(Greek/Roman), Baldur (Norse), Belenos (Celtic), Ra (Egyptian), Hades/Pluto (Greek/Roman), Horned God (Wicca)

Litha (The Summer Solstice)

Also called: Midsummer, or Midsummer's Eve

Celebrated: June 21–22 in the Northern Hemisphere and December 21–22 in the Southern Hemisphere

Litha celebrates the longest day of the year and the death of the Sun or victory of the Holly King. The strength of the God is strongest on this day.

Qualities: Strength, the Sun, vitality, growth

Deities: The Mother (Wicca), Áine (Celtic), Amaunet (Egyptian), Anuket (Egyptian), Aphrodite/Venus (Greek/Roman), Artemis/Diana (Greek/Roman), Athena/Minerva (Greek/Roman), Eos/Aurora (Greek/Roman), Bast (Egyptian), Fauna/Bona Dea (Greek/Roman), Brighid (Celtic), Cerridwen (Celtic), Epona/Rhiannon (Celtic), Frigga (Norse), Gaia/Terra (Greek/Roman), Hathor (Egyptian), Hera/Juno (Greek/Roman), Hestia/Vesta (Greek/Roman), Ra (Egyptian), Apollo (Greek/Roman), Baldur (Norse), Belenos (Celtic), Helios/Sol (Greek/Roman), Hodur (Norse), Janus (Roman), Lugh (Celtic), Zeus/Jupiter (Greek/Roman), Odin (Norse), Thor (Norse), Horned God (Wicca)

Lammas

Also called: Lughnasadh, Harvest Home, or First Harvest

Celebrated: August 1 in the Northern Hemisphere and February 1 in the Southern Hemisphere

Lughnasadh is the first of the three harvest Sabbats, honoring the time when the God begins to lose his energy.

Qualities: Abundance, creativity, gratitude

Deities: The Mother or the Wise Woman (Wicca), Isis (Egyptian), Demeter/Ceres (Greek/Roman), Nemesis/Invidia (Greek/Roman), Hathor (Egyptian), Hecate/Hekate (Greek/Roman), Artemis/Diana (Greek/Roman), Rhea/Ops (Greek/ Roman), Pomona (Roman), Danu (Celtic), Apollo (Greek/Roman), Osiris (Egyptian), Lugh (Celtic), Thor (Norse), Hephaestus/Vulcan (Greek/Roman), Loki (Norse), Horned God (Wicca)

Mabon (The Fall Equinox)

Also called: Autumn or Fall Equinox, Harvest Home, or Witch's Thanksgiving

Celebrated: September 22–23 in the Northern Hemisphere and March 20–21 in the Southern Hemisphere

During this second of three harvest Sabbat, the hours of day and night will be equal. Mabon also represents the Crone Goddess at full power.

Qualities: Abundance, balance, gratitude, protection, shadow work

Deities: The Wise Woman or the Crone (Wicca), Cerridwen (Celtic), Demeter/Ceres (Greek/Roman), Hecate/Hekate (Greek/Roman), Hera/Juno (Greek/Roman), Athena/Minerva (Greek/Roman), Persephone/Proserpina (Greek/Roman), Apollo (Greek/Roman), Dionysus/Bacchus (Greek/Roman), Green Man (Celtic), Hermes/Mercury (Greek/Roman), Zeus/Jupiter (Greek/Roman), Thor (Norse), Thoth (Egyptian), Hephaestus/Vulcan (Greek/Roman), Horned God (Wicca)

Samhain (All Hallows' Eve)

Also called: Hallowmas, Day of the Dead, All Hallows Eve, or Witch's New Year

Celebrated: October 31 in the Northern Hemisphere and April 30 in the Southern Hemisphere

Samhain, the third harvest Sabbat, is a time when the veil between life and death is thin, just like Beltane. Many use this time to honor their deceased friends, pets, and ancestors, and to work with spirits. Samhain also represents the death of the God in preparation for rebirth at Yule.

Qualities: Life, death, endings, shadow work

Deities: The Crone (Wicca), Cerridwen (Celtic), Demeter/Ceres (Greek/Roman), Hecate/Hekate (Greek/Roman), Hel (Norse), Isis (Egyptian), Morrighan (Celtic), Persephone/Proserpina (Greek/Roman), Pomona (Roman), Epona/Rhiannon (Celtic), Cernnunos (Celtic), Dagda (Celtic), Hades/Pluto (Greek/Roman), Janus (Roman), Osiris (Egyptian), Horned God (Wicca)

What Sabbat traditions would you like to try?

_____

_____

_____

_____

_____

The Esbats

Wiccans celebrate the monthly moon cycle during Esbats, or full moon rituals. These rituals honor the Goddess and her aspects of Maiden, Mother, and Crone. The name Esbat is derived from Old French *s'esbattre*, meaning "to frolic and amuse oneself." In Modern Wicca, most Esbats are celebrated in circles, sometimes called Goddess circles.

Celebrating an Esbat is the ideal way to connect to the Goddess and her aspects. If you work with other pantheons, each full moon also corresponds with other goddesses. In addition to celebrating the full moon, some Wiccans also hold new moon rituals. While the moon is linked with the Goddess, some practitioners may also honor the God and his aspects.

Each month's full moon has its own name, as well as additional names in other traditions. I have listed their common Wiccan names, as well as the Native American and Celtic names of each moon.

Most years have 12 full moons; however, because the Gregorian calendar is a solar calendar, it doesn't quite align with the lunar calendar and every once in a while, a year has a 13th full moon, called a Blue Moon.

Cold Moon (January)

Also called: Wolf moon (Native American), Birch moon (Celtic)

Qualities: Protection, intuition, wisdom

Deities: The Crone (Wicca), Freyja (Norse), Hera/Juno (Greek/Roman), Morrighan (Celtic), Hecate/Hekate (Greek/Roman)

Quickening Moon (February)

Also called: Snow or Hunger moon (Native American), Rowan moon (Celtic)

Qualities: Purification, growth, healing

Deities: The Maiden (Wicca), Aphrodite/Venus (Greek/Roman), Brighid (Celtic), Artemis/Diana (Greek/Roman), Demeter/Ceres (Greek/Roman), Hera/Juno (Greek/Roman), Persephone/Proserpina (Greek/Roman)

Storm Moon (March)

Also called: Chaste moon (common), Worm moon (Native American), Ash moon (Celtic)

Qualities: Rebirth, awakening

Deities: The Maiden (Wicca), Eostre (Norse/Germanic), Isis (Egyptian), Morrighan (Celtic), Artemis/Diana (Greek/Roman)

Wind Moon (April)

Also called: Seed moon (common), Flower or Pink moon (Native American), Alder moon (Celtic)

Qualities: Change, balance, emotions, planning

Deities: The Maiden (Wicca), Hathor (Egyptian), Demeter/Ceres (Greek/Roman), Aphrodite/Venus (Greek/Roman), Bast (Egyptian)

Flower Moon (May)

Also called: Milk or Planting moon (Native American), Willow moon (Celtic)

Qualities: Building energy, intuition, commitments, connections

Deities: The Mother (Wicca), Bast (Egyptian), Aphrodite/Venus (Greek/ Roman), Artemis/Diana (Greek/Roman)

Sun Moon (June)

Also called: Rose or Honey moon (common), Strawberry moon (Native American), Hawthorn moon (Celtic)

Qualities: Protection, strengthening, preventive, endurance

Deities: The Mother (Wicca), Isis (Egyptian), Cerridwen (Celtic), Hera/ Juno (Greek/Roman), Persephone/Proserpina (Greek/Roman)

Blessing Moon (July)

Also called: Buck or Deer moon (common), Hay or Thunder moon (Native American), Oak moon (Celtic)

Qualities: Divination, dream work, psychic abilities, home, repairing

Deities: The Mother (Wicca), Hera/Juno (Greek/Roman), Cerridwen (Celtic), Aphrodite/Venus (Greek/Roman), Athena/Minerva (Greek/Roman)

Corn Moon (August)

Also called: Sturgeon or Fish moon (common), Red moon (Native American), Holly or Hazel moon (Celtic)

Qualities: Rebirth, abundance, prosperity, renewal

Deities: The Wise Woman or the Mother (Wicca), Nemesis/Invidia (Greek/Roman), Hecate/Hekate (Greek/Roman), Hathor (Egyptian)

Harvest Moon (September)

Also called: Fruit moon (Native American), Vine moon (Celtic)

Qualities: Balance, emotions, meditation, mental and physical well-being

Deities: The Wise Woman or the Crone (Wicca), Demeter/Ceres (Greek/Roman), Isis (Egyptian), Freyja (Norse)

Blood Moon (October)

Also called: Falling Leaf moon (common), Hunter's moon (Native American), Ivy moon (Celtic)

Qualities: Letting go, cleansing, karma, growth, divination, dream work, spirits

Deities: The Wise Woman or the Crone (Wicca), Demeter/Ceres (Greek/Roman), Morrighan (Celtic)

Mourning Moon (November)

Also called: Frost or Beaver moon (Native American), Reed moon (Celtic)

Qualities: Shedding habits or relationships, fresh starts, connections

Deities: The Crone (Wicca), Isis (Egyptian), Hecate/Hekate (Greek/Roman), Bast (Egyptian), Skadi (Norse)

Long Nights Moon (December)

Also called: Cold moon (Native American), Elder moon (Celtic)

Qualities: Endurance, rebirth, transformation

Deities: The Crone (Wicca), Hathor (Egyptian), Hecate/Hekate (Greek/Roman), Athena/Minerva (Greek/Roman), Persephone/Proserpina (Greek/Roman), Norns (Norse)

Blue Moon (13th)

Also called: the fourth full moon of a season

Qualities: Amplifier

Deities: Artemis/Diana (Greek/Roman), Hecate/Hekate (Greek/Roman), Selene/Luna (Greek/Roman), Triple Goddess (Wicca)

Which Esbat traditions do you practice or would like to try?

_____

_____

_____

_____

_____

Sacred Runes

If you're drawn to the Norse pantheon, you'll probably be interested in working with sacred runes. Runes are an ancient Germanic alphabet that pre-dates Latin, but they're much more than just one of the earliest written languages. The word _rune_ is derived from the Old English word _rūn,_ meaning "a secret hidden lore." Runes are secrets, much like the "arcana" in tarot. There are layers of meaning and messages hidden with each rune symbol.

But although people working with the Norse pantheon might be especially interested in runes, that is absolutely not a requirement. Anyone can gain access to runes and use them in their practice. For centuries, pagans have used the runic alphabet for both writing and in divination. Today, there are some Wiccans who even use the runic alphabet to write their Book of Shadows.

The Elder Futhark are both the oldest type of runes and the most popular form used in paganism today. There are 24 runes in the Elder Futhark, divided into three groups of eight runes called an "ætt" —Old Norse meaning "division." In the magical community, there will often be mention of a 25th symbol or "blank" rune. This isn't historically backed, but it's a personal choice if you feel called to use it.

Freyja's Ætt

These runes represent a personal awakening, the beginning of the universe, order out of chaos, and the creation of all things.

Name	Letter	Symbol	Meaning	Qualities
Fehu (Fay-who)	F	ᚠ	Cattle	Wealth, power, control, nourishment, possessions
Uruz (Ooo-roounc-ese)	U	ᚢ	Auroch	Strength, endurance, change, burdens, sacrifices, risks, patience
Thurisaz (Thor-is-as)	Th	ᚦ	Giant	Defense, thorns, protection, chaos
Ansuz (Ann-suhz)	A	ᚨ	God	Learning, communication, guidance
Raidho (Ride-ho)	R	ᚱ	Wagon, ride	Journey, wheel, ride, travel, progress
Kenaz (Keh-nawz)	K,C	ᚲ	Torch, knowledge	Inner wisdom, success, light, guidance
Gebo (Ghe-bow)	G	ᚷ	Gift	Giving, partnership, generosity, marriage, balance
Wunjo (Woon-yo)	V, W	ᚹ	Joy	Happiness, joy, harmony, good news

Heimdall's Ætt

These runes represent the realities and external forces that cause change in the energies established in the first ætt.

Name	Letter	Symbol	Meaning	Qualities
Hagalaz (Hag-all-az)	H	ᚺ	Hail	Radical change, crisis, storm, transformation
Nauthiz (Nah-deez)	N	ᚾ	Need	Lessons, desire, thoughts, necessity, limitations
Isa (Iss-ah)	I	ᛁ	Ice	Stillness, patience, control, challenges, delay
Jera (Yehr-ah)	J, Y	ᛃ	Year, cycle	Cycle, ending, new beginning, accomplishments, reward
Ihwaz, Eihwaz (Eye-waz)	Y	ᛇ	Yew tree	Endings, rebirth, death, longevity, endurance
Perthro (Per-throw)	P	ᛈ	Unknown	Mystery, secret, luck, choices
Algiz (All-yeese)	Z	ᛉ	Elk	Protection, healing, growth, success
Sowilo (Soe-wee-low)	S	ᛊ	Sun	Guidance, success, hope, confidence, expansion

Tyr's Ætt

These runes help us deal with the external forces of the second ætt as we travel the path outlined in the first ætt.

Name	Letter	Symbol	Meaning	Qualities
Tiwaz (Tea-waz)	T	↑	God Tyr	Self-sacrifice, loyalty, justice, balance
Berkano (Burr-can-oh)	B	ᛒ	Birch Goddess	Beginnings, growth, birth, fertility
Ehwaz (Eh-was)	E	ᛗ	Horse	Teamwork, trust
Mannaz (Man-az)	M	ᛗ	Mankind	Self, inner being, creativity
Laguz (Log-uhz)	L	ᚱ	Lake	Water, unconscious, dreams, journey, intuition
Inguz (Ing-guz)	Ng	◇	God Ing, seed	Action, internal growth, transformation, awareness, love, development
Dagaz (Day-gahz)	D	ᛞ	Day	Awakening, daylight, light, cycles, endings, beginnings, optimism
Othala (Oh-thall-ah)	O	ᛟ	Homeland	Home, possession, inheritance, ancestry, family

Rune Stones

A set of stones with a different rune etched onto each stone is used to divine messages. To read the stones, "cast" them—meaning, shake the bag they're carried in, and then gently throw the stones onto a surface. If you prefer, you can also read rune cards, which are read in a similar fashion to tarot, oracle, or other divination card systems.

To get to know the runes, I recommend making your own rune stones by venturing into nature, collecting some stones, and marking them with a permanent marker. If you don't have access to stones, wood chips or shells can also be used.

Rune Stone Readings

Before using any runes for the first time, you'll want to cleanse them. Cleansing them allows them to be "reset" for use, so they can be attuned to your specific energy. The easiest way to do this is by utilizing one of the elements. You can use smoke from incense for air, warmth from a candle flame for fire, spring or distilled water for water, or salt for earth.

To begin a reading, set your intentions and think clearly about your spread. Shake your bag of stones, then close your eyes as you pull out three runes, one at a time. The left rune is the past, the center rune represents the present, and the right rune is the future.

Grab your runes to practice casting! Record your first few readings in the box that follows.

My Readings

Hallowed Sigils

Another powerful form of symbolism in Wicca is the sigil. The term *sigil* comes from the Latin *sigillum,* meaning "sign." Sigils are physical representations of intentions or desires that are unique to the practitioner and can be quickly created with a pencil and paper.

To create your own sigils, follow these steps:

1. Decide what your intentions are, whether they relate to luck, love, prosperity, or protection.

2. Write down a sentence about your intentions on a piece of paper.

3. Begin crossing out or erasing all the vowels in the sentence.

4. Cross out or erase any duplicate consonants.

5. Take the remaining letters and fit them together in any creative way that feels right to you. This includes either layering the letters into a single symbol, or leaving the letters as they are. Sigils are your own creations.

Another way to create a sigil is by using shapes that already have meanings. This can include runes, zodiac signs, glyphs, shapes like hearts, or the elements. Both methods will allow you to create custom sigils for use in your practice.

Once you have created your new sigil, it can be etched, carved, or marked onto an object to infuse it with your sigil's intentions.

Think about your intentions, then use the space below to create your first sigil.

Wiccan Symbols

Whether they are sigils, alphabets, or unique designs you create, symbols hold power. Carving symbols or sigils into candles is one of the most popular ways to activate and use their power, but there are countless ways to incorporate symbols into your Book of Shadows, your altar, and your tools. Below is a list of common Wiccan symbols, but it's far from definitive. If you follow other pantheons, you'll also have symbols of those faiths.

Pentagram: A five-pointed star often used on altars to represent Wicca or witchcraft. The points often refer to the five elements for altar work.

Pentacle: A pentagram enclosed within a circle. This is often seen in tarot.

Deosil and Widdershins: The directions of energy during altar work. Deosil, from the Gaelic *dei-seil*, is to move clockwise while widdershins, from Middle Low German *weddersinnes*, means "against the way," to move counterclockwise.

Elemental Triangles: A set of four different triangles representing air, earth, fire, and water. A circle represents the fifth element of spirit.

Horned God: Often depicted in a glyph similar to Taurus, or a circle with a crescent to create antlers on a head. Also called the God or the Lord.

Triple Goddess: A set of three moons—waxing, full, and waning—used to symbolize the Maiden, Mother, and Crone aspects of the all-encompassing Wiccan Goddess. Also called the Lady, or the Goddess.

Sun Cross or Solar Cross: A four-arm cross enclosed in a circle representing not only the Sun, but also the cyclical nature of the seasons.

Wheel of the Year: An eight-arm sun cross to represent the eight Sabbats.

Triquetra or Trinity Knot: An ancient Celtic symbol representing the Triple Goddess, the cycle of life, death, and rebirth, and protection.

Ogham Staves

If you have an interest in the Celtic pantheon, you'll most likely come across Ogham, the earliest known form of Gaelic. The Ogham alphabet consists of 20 letters, each of which also represents a Celtic tree. Ogham staves—sticks with each letter inscribed on them—have layers of meaning, just like runes and other symbols found in Wicca.

Name	Letter	Symbol	Tree	Qualities
Beith	B		Birch	New beginnings, change, release, rebirth
Luis	L		Rowan	Insight, protection, blessings, inspiration
Fearn	F		Alder	Renewal, healing, evolving
Saille	S		Willow	Rhythms of life, growth, knowledge
Nion	N		Ash	Inner self, outer worlds, travel
Huath	H		Hawthorn	Fertility, cleansing, protection, defense
Duir	D		Oak	Power, strength, doorways, self-confidence
Tinne	T		Holly	Unity, courage, stability, life

Name	Letter	Symbol	Tree	Qualities
Coll	C		Hazel	Wisdom, knowledge, creativity, divination
Quert	Q		Apple	Love, faithfulness, rebirth
Muin	M		Blackberry	Lessons, learning, truth, instincts
Gort	G		Ivy	Growth, searching, visions
Ngeatal	Ng		Reed	Health, healing, gatherings
Straith	St		Blackthorn	Fertility, control, authority, secrets, struggles
Ruis	R		Elder	Time, endings, maturity, knowledge
Ailim	A		Elm	Rising above, clear vision

Name	Letter	Symbol	Tree	Qualities
Onn	O		Gorse	Renewal, purification, inspiration
Uhr	U		Heather	Self-discovery, messengers, healing
Eadhadh	E		Aspen	Endurance, courage, protection
Iodhadh	I		Yew	Rebirth, death, beginnings, cycles

You can make your own staves to use for readings and divination. To start, find small sticks that you can carve or dowel rods. Sand the bark on each stick so that it's smooth. Inscribe each of the sticks with one of the Ogham symbols above.

Before using your Ogham staves for the first time, you'll want to cleanse them using an element, just as you did with your runes. To begin a reading, set your intentions and think clearly about your question. Shake your bag of staves, then close your eyes and pull out one. Pull one stave each morning for daily guidance. This daily practice is also a great way to get to know the staves.

Buy some Ogham staves or make your own, and then practice casting. Make notes on your readings or daily pulls in the space below.

PART II

SPELLS, RITUALS, AND RECIPES FOR A THOROUGHLY WICCAN LIFE

I t's now time to begin putting our knowledge into action. Before diving into the practical aspects of Wicca, including spells, rituals, recipes, and candle magic, let's cover some of the most important aspects of preparation. After covering intention setting, altars, and tools, we'll get into spellwork. Each section has blank, customizable sections to personalize with your own ingredient lists, notes, and spells.

CHAPTER 3

Finding Your Inner Magic and Other Preparations for Practice

In this chapter, you'll learn how to set intentions, cast circles for protection, set up an altar, and take the first steps to prepare for your spellwork. All these practices and rituals are adaptable: I'll share the basics and why they're important, but it's up to you to decide what you want to implement in your own practice and why.

The Wiccan Within

Beginning to call yourself a Wiccan isn't as complicated as you'd think. You can become Wiccan simply by making a choice to venture down the Wiccan path. That choice is the first step, followed by defining your beliefs and desire to learn. Many Wiccans then choose to perform a self-dedication ritual—a formal declaration of your intentions to join the Wiccan path.

How would you describe your Wiccan identity? If you want to develop a self-dedication ritual, what would you want it to include?

_____

_____

_____

_____

_____

The Importance of Intention and Centering the Self

Intentions are key when performing rituals, spells, or other magical workings. They are the wishes or goals of your practice and the reason you cast. Without setting clear intentions, you're opening your practice to unclear and muddled wishes, which could backfire in unexpected ways. It's important to be clear about what you want and why.

Centering and grounding the self is just as important as setting intentions. Centering allows you to alter your mental and physical state through energy and visualization. It's feeling calm, in control, and in balance during your practice. Skipping out on centering can leave you feeling lost or out of touch with your emotions, body, or spirit. Grounding goes hand in hand with centering and allows you to release built-up or excess energy, so you don't feel jittery or anxious after your rituals or spells.

Successful intention setting and centering can lead to the manifestation of your goals, positive changes in your life, and connection to your intuition.

Setting Intentions

To manifest or attract your intended outcome, take time before your rituals, spellwork, or other magic to create a few goals. Two easy ways to get started setting intentions are through visualization and journaling, which can be used together or separately. During the next Esbat or Sabbat, use the visualization and journaling techniques below to help set clear intentions to manifest your goals.

Visualization allows you to see yourself performing a ritual or task with an outcome you desire before physically performing your task. To begin visualization, allow yourself 10 minutes for sitting and relaxing, focusing on your breathing. Then, picture yourself performing your task. Describe what you want and create the emotions along with it to improve your intentions. This allows your visualization to come to life, giving you a clear idea of what you want and why. Setting intentions with visualization is perfect for rituals, spellwork, and energy magic.

Journaling is a great way to write down your thoughts and ideas in order to set clear intentions, making them more attainable and less intimidating. Journaling is tangible and easy to reference when you need to focus and repeat. Setting intentions with journaling is very powerful and ideal for recipes, divination, sigils, or other physical magic.

Centering and Grounding the Self

Centering is when you reinforce your connection to yourself, bringing your energy into focus to help you feel more balanced. By centering, you are focusing on your relationship to your energy, which will help you work with it. Centering often goes hand in hand with grounding, because these two techniques help you stay balanced and at energy equilibrium. It's important to center and ground yourself when you feel restless, overwhelmed, unfocused, forgetful, or like your self-esteem is low.

The easiest way to center is through meditation and visualization. Find a quiet place to sit and begin with long, slow, deep breaths, in and out. Once you feel relaxed and at peace, you can visualize your energy. Gently rub your hands together and slowly pull them apart, focusing on the space between them. Any tingling sensations you feel are threads of energy waiting to be used. If you're having a hard time with this, hold a crystal instead of rubbing your hands and visualize energy pooling in the crystal. You should feel the crystal get hot; this is the energy building. Now you can use the energy for your practice, in ritual, spells, recipes, or other magical workings.

After you have finished, it's time to ground any excess energy to bring yourself back to balance. I recommend that beginners use grounding crystals such as hematite, moonstone, obsidian, and sodalite to assist with this process. Sit in a comfortable position and begin focusing on your breath. Next, visualize all the excess energy you've built leaving your body and returning to the Earth.

How do intentions fit into your practice? Which forms of centering and grounding are most effective for you?

Casting and Opening a Magical Circle

Casting and opening a magical circle means creating a boundary of energy for protection during ritual or magical workings. "Opening a circle" is also called "closing a circle" depending on who you've learned from. For this book, I'll use the term *opening*.

Not all Wiccans cast magical circles. They are very much optional, but some practitioners like them. I use them because circles can help separate the mundane from the magical. I like to think of a magical circle as a switch that's flipped to "on" when my ritual or spell is in progress. The casting of a circle creates a sacred space that assists with blocking unwanted energy or attention. Plus, the protection of the circle is often comforting. They are especially helpful for meditation and rituals that need focus and peace. Circles can also be marked physically by candles, salt, crystals, or other objects that are imbued with energy or represent the elements.

Casting a magical circle involves moving clockwise and calling the quarters, directions, or elements to surround you. To cast a circle, you may hold an energy amplifier such as a wand or athame to assist with directing energy. Then, face the easternmost point and say something along the lines of: *"Element of air, with your gentle breeze, join me and lend me your mental clarity."*

Next, you may turn to the south and say: *"Element of fire, with your warming light, ignite and lend me your energy."*

Turning to the west, you may say: *"Element of water, with your rolling tides, lend me your fluidity."*

Finally, you may return to the north and say: *"Element of earth, with your grounding surface, lend me your stability."*

To include the fifth element of spirit, say something like: *"With these elements together under spirit, I cast a circle of protection above, below, within."*

Once your magical circle is cast, move on to your magical workings. Once you're finished with the main part of your ritual, open your circle to release the energy back to nature.

The process of opening a circle begins counterclockwise, starting from the north. To release earth, say something along the lines of: *"Earth, I thank you for your assistance and bid you farewell."*

Next, turn to the west to release water: *"Water, I thank you for your assistance and bid you farewell."*

Then, you'll turn to the south to release fire: *"Fire, I thank you for your assistance and bid you farewell."*

After that, you'll turn to the east to release air: *"Air, I thank you for your assistance and bid you farewell."*

Finally, you'll return back north to release spirit and the magical circle by saying something like: *"Spirit, I bid you farewell. I open this circle and release the energy back into the Earth."*

When the circle is opened, you should expect to feel grounded and relaxed.

The steps you use to cast and open a circle are also entirely adaptable and optional. You can change the incantations to something more poetic or rewrite them altogether. Some Wiccans will also change the starting location to the north instead of east. This is up to the preference of the practitioner. What is important is speaking from your heart and being true to your practice.

Do you think a magical circle might have a place in your practice? If so, what steps, incantations, or directions would you want to use when casting it?

_____

_____

_____

_____

_____

_____

_____

_____

Tools for the Wiccan Witch

In Wicca, there are many tools you can choose to use to amplify your spells and rituals. Most of them aren't required, but if you feel drawn to them, they can make your practice more personal and powerful. You can find most of these tools at in-person or online metaphysical shops, as well as on Etsy and eBay. You can also create your own versions, using household materials or items from craft stores. These tools are uniquely yours, so get as creative, extravagant, or thrifty as you'd like with them.

Below, you'll find a list of popular Wiccan tools, what they're often made from, and the easiest way to make or source them.

Athame/Wand/Ritual Knife

An athame, wand, or ritual knife is used as an extension of your hand during rituals, to help direct energy. Athames and ritual knives aren't dangerous like regular knives—their edges are typically blunt. Wands are often crafted from various types of wood. Many Wiccans add or attach crystals or stones to their athame, wand, or ritual knife to amplify energy. You can make your own athame with a simple household knife. Wrap the handle in clay or wire, and personalize it using hot glue, crystals, and paint.

Bells

Bells are very versatile—they can be used to call upon deity, banish negative energy, create harmony, and generate power through sound and vibration. Many practitioners incorporate them into circle casting, purification, and spirit work. It's easy to source bells from craft stores or old holiday decorations.

Bowls

Wooden or metal bowls are often used to hold salt, incense, herbs, crystals, and water during ritual work. You can use bowls purchased from any home goods store. For some witchy flair, you can also use a cauldron or a cast-iron pot as your bowl.

Broom

A broom, also called a besom, isn't just for cleaning up. It can sweep the old energies of previous spellwork or rituals away from an altar space or room. Many Wiccans also use a miniature besom to clean and clear their altar and tools. Though any broom can work as a besom, make sure that you don't also use it for cleaning the house—this should be a dedicated tool. You can make your own mini-besom by wrapping twigs or hardy herbs with twine or ribbon.

Candles

Candles are as varied as the spells and rituals they're used in. They come in every color, shape, and size, and can be made from beeswax, paraffin wax, gel, or plant waxes such as carnauba, palm, soybean, or bayberry. If you're beginning your practice, I recommend tea light or votive candles, because they are quicker to burn and can be used for single-use ritual work. When purchasing candles, always look at the average burn time to coordinate with your meditations, rituals, recipes, or spells. You don't want to use a candle that will burn down midway through your spell.

Candles can be found at metaphysical shops, craft stores, some grocery stores, and online retailers. On websites like Etsy, you can find practitioners selling spell candles, as well as materials for creating your own. I'll be sharing more about candle colors, sizes, and spells for candle magic in chapter 6.

Cauldron

Cauldrons are large pots, similar to chalices or bowls used on the altar. They relate to the Lady or Goddess and, in the Celtic pantheon, are a symbol of the Goddess Cerridwen. Cauldrons are often made from cast iron and are fire safe. Many Wiccans have multiple cauldrons for different uses—for instance, one is used for burning herbs and paper, while another is dedicated to preparing liquids you intend to consume. You can find cauldrons online or at metaphysical shops.

Censer

A censer is an incense burner that holds charcoal for burning loose incense or resins. Censers are often burned before and during circle casting or at the beginning of rituals. They come in many different designs, are fire-resistant, and are often made of iron, brass, ceramic, or clay. You can find a censer online or at a metaphysical shop.

Chalice/Ritual Cup

A chalice or ritual cup is a goblet used to hold beverages such as water, wine, or tea during ritual or cake and ale ceremonies. The chalice represents the element of water; it also, like the bowl and cauldron, represents the Goddess. You can find ritual cups and chalices online, at Goodwill, or at home decor stores.

Crystals

Crystals are used for healing, manifestation, assisting with energy, and representing the element of earth. They can also be utilized for divination and crystal grids, and incorporated into athame handles, wands, or pentacles to amplify their energy. Some Wiccans use crystals to physically mark the boundary for casting a circle.

The easiest way to start working with crystals is to get clear quartz, which can be used in place of any other crystal. You can find crystals in nature, online, and at craft and metaphysical stores.

Every crystal is unique, so a guidebook or list of crystal correspondences can be handy when choosing which stones you require.

Crystal Ball/Scrying Mirror

Crystal balls and scrying mirrors are tools for divination practices like scrying or gazing. Scrying involves gazing into a smooth, reflective surface. Doing so allows you to receive messages, visions, or images to interpret intuitively. The age-old image of a fortune-teller gazing into a crystal ball is a classic example of scrying. Scrying during ritual is a great way to harness the built-up energy. Crystals, water, smoke, flame, or mirrors are all surfaces that can be used to scry. Scrying mirrors can be bought or made by applying black paint on a mirror or plate. Crystal balls are most often found at metaphysical shops or online.

Herbs and Essential Oils

Using herbs and oils in your practice can help you become closer to nature. Every herb has magical properties that work in tandem with your intentions, allowing your creativity to thrive in rituals, recipes, and spells. Essential oils contain plant essences and properties, making them a great option if you want to incorporate fragrance or mix several herbs. Teas and infused oils are some of the easiest ways to incorporate these ingredients into your routine.

Herbs can be grown at home or purchased from supermarkets, farmers' markets, and online retailers, or by searching for reputable sources. Make sure that any herbs you use internally are food-grade. It's also very important to make sure that any essential oils you use are diluted in a carrier oil such as jojoba, coconut, or olive—full-strength essential oils can irritate your skin. I'll be sharing more about herb profiles, essential oil properties, and recipes you can make in chapter 5.

Tarot and Oracle Cards

Tarot and oracle cards are popular because they empower you to listen to your intuition. Oracle decks, which come in sets of 20 to 80 cards, can often be used directly out of the box with no training, which makes them ideal for beginners. Tarot is a more advanced divination system consisting of 78 cards, divided into the major and minor arcana. The major arcana represent significant life events, while the minor arcana represent the day-to-day. It takes a lot of time and effort to learn the tarot, but if your intuition is strong, you may be able to jump right in. When picking out a deck, allow your intuition to guide you in choosing something that calls to you.

Which tools are you most drawn to? Makes notes here for your Wiccan tool wish list.

_____

_____

_____

_____

_____

_____

_____

_____

_____

_____

_____

_____

_____

_____

_____

Clearing, Consecrating, and Charging Your Tools

Once you have begun collecting and creating the tools you want to use in your practice, it's time to start clearing, consecrating, and charging them.

Clearing, also sometimes called cleansing, refers to cleaning a tool both physically and spiritually. Depending on the tool's material, you can clear it by washing it with water, cleansing it with smoke, sprinkling salt on it, or sweeping a besom over it.

Consecrating means making the tool sacred for ritual or use. To consecrate your tools, you'll first need to set your intentions. You can also use the elements to assist in infusing their energy into your tools. To do this, use objects that represent the elements—salt for earth, smoke for air, a candle for fire, or a bowl of liquid for water—and pass them through each of the elements while asking for assistance.

Charging refers to empowering or building energy. It can be done by holding the tool and visualizing, chanting, or meditating. To infuse it with solar or lunar energy, you can leave a tool out under the full moon or the sun to absorb its power. Crystals hold energy like batteries, so it's a great idea to charge your crystals monthly—then you can use them in rituals at any time of the month.

These processes allow old energies to be purified. Old energies can interfere with your rituals and spells, causing unwanted side effects.

Follow these easy steps whenever you get a new tool:

1. Rinse or clean the surface of your tool.

2. Use water, smoke, salt, or your besom to purify and cleanse your tool.

3. To consecrate using the elements, pass the tool through the representation of each element and call upon that element for

assistance. You can also consecrate with anointing oils or by calling upon deity.

4. Hold the tool in your hands and visualize, chant, or meditate your intentions.

5. Optional: Leave the tool out under the sun or full moon to charge.

Building Your Wiccan Altar

An altar, also known as your practice workspace, is a surface, table, or area that's used solely for rituals, spells, and other magical workings. You can store your magical tools, spells, and offerings there, along with deity and elemental representations. Similar to a magical circle, this space allows you to separate the magical from the mundane. Many Wiccans also redecorate their altars each month or season in order to reflect their practice or intentions.

On a Wiccan's altar, you'll often find a Book of Shadows, chalice, athame, besom, incense, pentacle, cauldron, wand, crystals, and candles. These tools are popular because of their practical use as well as their relation to the elements. Athames and incense are often chosen to represent air; wands and candles represent fire; chalices and cauldrons represent water; and pentacles and crystals represent earth. Candles can also represent deity and the elements.

The layout of your altar can be methodical, intuitive, or free from structure. A common layout places deity in the top-most center area, with elemental representations laid out according to their location— earth representations in the north, air in the east, fire in the south, water in the west, and spirit in the center.

An alternate layout places your elemental items according to their position in a pentacle. The topmost center point represents spirit. Then, moving in a clockwise direction, water is set next, then fire, then earth, then air. You can follow these layouts or create your own. When deciding what's right for you, it's important to note that the power of an altar and its tools doesn't come from adhering to a certain layout—it comes from the meanings and intentions you invest in it.

Draw your ideal altar in the box that follows, then make notes about the placements, tools, and themes that most interest you.

Cleansing Your Sacred Space

Now that you've planned out your altar, you'll want to cleanse it and the space around it. Just as it's important to clear your tools, you'll also want to cleanse your altar and space in order to remove unwanted or negative energy and make it sacred. You can achieve this by using censers or smudge sticks to waft smoke over the space or using a besom or broom to sweep away the energies. If your space allows it, you can also use distilled and charged water, or sprinkle salt.

CHAPTER 4

Spell Crafting

With the basics out of the way, we can now dive into the practical side of magic. In this section, I'll introduce you to a number of spells, including ones for love, prosperity, health, and protection. You'll also create some brand-new spells that are all your own—there is space to write them down at the end of each section.

Before we get started, please note that if you plan on casting a magical circle for these spells, do so after step one, and open the circle after the last step.

The spells presented in this book are intended for solitary practice, for more of a personal experience. However, you can apply much of the information you learn here to future group practice, too, if you so choose.

Creating Your Own Spells

To create your own spells, you'll need to set clear intentions. Once you have a clear goal or desire in mind, you can begin collecting ingredients. This is where the fun and creativity really begin. Perform a simple search to find herbs, flowers, stones, runes, symbols, colors, or other materials and tools that align with your spell's properties. A spell can take anywhere from 10 to 30 minutes. It all depends on how you perform your steps and the time you take.

Now get ready to use your altar, tools, and intentions to create the changes you want to make in your life.

Spells for Love, Friendship, and Other Relationships

In this section, there are easy spells you can try or adapt for matters around the heart, from love to friendship. I hope these spells can inspire your future spells. Use the templates throughout this section to write your own spells. Enjoy performing these spells, whether you're in love or looking to mend bonds. To cast these spells at their strongest, perform them on a Friday, the day ruled by Venus and love deities. To create your own spells for love, friendship, and other relationships, you'll need to set clear intentions. Once you have a clear goal or desire in mind, you can begin collecting ingredients. This is where the fun and creativity take place. By performing a simple search, you can find herbs, flowers, stones, runes, symbols, colors, or other materials and tools that align with your spell's properties.

For the three spells I've included, I chose a simple friendship pendant charm spell, a honey love attraction spell, and a relationship meditation spell. The friendship pendant charm spell is an easy, minimalistic spell anyone can perform. The honey love attraction spell amplifies honey magic, which contains properties of love and courage while also being very viscous. Honey is excellent for binding and attracting magick. For the third spell, I chose to focus on aligning with your emotions through meditation. I've included optional additions like incense and music to help set the mood. This is a straightforward spell to get started with, as it doesn't require many materials.

Friendship Pendant
Charm Spell

Focus on your intentions of friendship as you build energy to imbue with a pendant. This simple spell can be used on a single necklace or multiple. Use it for strengthening friendships and long-lasting bonds. Recharge your pendant periodically. To boost your spell, charge your clear quartz crystal under the moonlight or sunlight.

Time needed:
10 to 15 minutes

Ingredients/tools:
Pendant
Clear quartz crystal

1. Cleanse your altar and place the pendant in the center of your table.
2. Set your intentions for strengthening your friendship.
3. Hold the pendant in your dominant hand while you hold the clear quartz in the other. Close your eyes and focus on your breathing.
4. Feel energy build in the clear quartz crystal.
5. Next, concentrate on moving that energy to the pendant through your body.
6. Energy will surround the pendant and it will begin to warm in your hand.
7. Your pendant is charged and ready to be worn.

Honey Love Attraction Spell

Send out sweetening energy to attract love and feelings old and new in the world. Honey has long been used in love magic for romantic courage and long-lasting happiness because of its sweet properties.

Time needed:
15 minutes

Ingredients/tools:
Pen and paper
4-ounce glass jar and lid
3 ounces honey
1 tablespoon dried rose petals

1. Cleanse your altar and prepare your ingredients.
2. Set your intentions and write down your desire on the piece of paper.
3. Fold and place the paper in the jar and cover it with honey.
4. Slowly sprinkle dried rose petals into the honey.
5. Seal the jar and hold it between your hands to charge.

Relationship Meditation Spell

Align your perspective and regulate your emotions through a meditation spell. This is a simple spell that allows you to step outside yourself to get a fresh look at your relationships. Depending on your intentions, this spell can be used for partners, friends, or other loved ones.

Time needed:
30 minutes

Ingredients/tools:
Incense (stick, cone, or loose on a charcoal disk)
Lighter or match
Meditation music (optional)

1. Cleanse your meditation area, light your incense, and turn on music if you'd like any.
2. Sit or lie down in a comfortable position and begin focusing on your intentions.
3. Begin taking long, slow, deep breaths, inhaling and exhaling as you release any tension or tightness in your muscles.
4. Move your awareness to your heart and place your hand over it.
5. Visualize your relationship as clearly as you can, standing outside yourself.
6. Direct your thoughts to the relationship as you are now seeing it. Are you looking for understanding, truth, positivity, or acceptance? Say three kind statements about the relationship.
7. Return to your breathing, focusing on feeling lighter as you come back to awareness.

Spell title:

_____

_____

_____

Time needed:

_____

Ingredients/tools:

_____   _____

_____   _____

_____   _____

1. _____

2. _____

3. _____

4. _____

5. _____

6. _____

7. _____

Spell title:

_____

_____

_____

Time needed:

_____

Ingredients/tools:

_____ _____

_____ _____

_____ _____

1. _____

2. _____

3. _____

4. _____

5. _____

6. _____

7. _____

Spells for Prosperity and Abundance

In this section, enjoy spells focused on prosperity, both from material objects and immaterial. Pair them with your intentions of bringing prosperity to all aspects of your life as well as those around you. Use the templates that follow my spells to write your own spells.

To cast these spells at their strongest, perform them on a Thursday, the day ruled by Jupiter and prosperity deities. For adaptions and substitutions, look to work with the element of earth, the colors green, gold, or brown, and the deities for prosperity and abundance.

For the three spells I've included, I chose an abundance jar spell, a prosperity burn spell, and a make money sigil spell. The abundance jar is a great introductory way of formulating layered charms. The prosperity burn spell centers around burning bay leaves to communicate your intentions. For the third spell, I use the power of symbolism to help you create your sigil. The steps involved will allow you to be creative and also attract energy toward you.

Abundance Jar Spell

Attract energy of abundance to you with this layered jar charm and spell. You can have fun and tailor the ingredients to suit what you might already have on hand. This jar is filled with herbs and a crystal with abundance properties for infusing your intentions with power. The jar can be any size you have, or look at using old storage jars from your favorite foods. Just remember to thoroughly clean and clear your previously used objects.

Time needed:
10 to 15 minutes

Ingredients/tools:
Small glass jar
1 tablespoon basil
1 tablespoon mint
1 tablespoon chamomile
1 cinnamon stick or 1 tablespoon dried cinnamon powder
1 green crystal (emerald, green jade, citrine, clear quartz, or pyrite)

1. Cleanse your altar and prepare your ingredients.
2. Close your eyes, set your intentions, and visualize what it means to you to have abundance be attracted to you.
3. Hold that image in your mind's eye as you begin to layer your ingredients.
4. Fill the jar between half and three-quarters full with your herbs.
5. Hold the crystal in your hand to charge and connect with the energy.
6. Place the crystal in the jar, seal it, and place the sealed jar on your altar or somewhere near to attract abundance.

Prosperity Burn Spell

Bay leaves, when burned, can energetically carry your wishes and intentions out into the world. To adapt this spell, you can alter the quantity of bay leaves used or perform it outdoors for better ventilation. Fill in the blank in the incantation below to make it yours.

Time needed:
20 minutes

Ingredients/tools:
Black marker
Paper
Green or white candle and match or lighter
3 dried bay leaves
Cast-iron cauldron or fire-safe bowl

1. Cleanse your altar and prepare your materials.
2. Spend a few minutes setting your intentions. Meditate or visualize if desired.
3. Write down the prosperity energy you'd like to attract in one or two words. Is it wealth, security, comfort, success, or something different altogether? Fill in the blanks in the incantation below as well.
4. Light your candle or grab your lighter.
5. Set the corner of the first bay leaf on fire. When it catches, place it in the cauldron to burn.
6. As it burns you can say: *"Prosperity burning bay, with your flame, light the way, and bring to me _____."*
7. Repeat the incantation as you burn each of the next two bay leaves, *"Prosperity burning bay, with your flame, light the way, and bring to me _____."*

Make Money Sigil Spell

Use the magic of symbolism to boost money-attracting energy. Symbols are highly adaptable and unique to each practitioner. Sew, draw, etch, or carve sigils into objects, candles, or charms. The steps below can be adapted for every sigil you create. If you're using incense to assist with money energy, look to use cinnamon, clove, patchouli, jasmine, vanilla, or pine.

Time needed:

20 minutes

Ingredients/tools:

Incense (optional)
Lighter or match
Pen and paper
Object to draw the sigil on (stone, wood, cloth, etc.)

1. Cleanse your altar and light your incense.
2. Focus on your intentions as you think up a phrase or sentence for attracting money. To get started, you can use *"Make Money."*
3. Now take out all the vowels until you're left with *"Mkmny."*
4. Then, take out the repeating letters and you'll have *"Mkny."*
5. You can combine these letters in a symbol, or further divide the letters into lines and arcs before creating a symbol. There's no wrong way to create a symbol—this is where your creativity flourishes. Have fun and remember to think about your intentions.
6. Draw your finished sigil onto your object, then charge it by holding it in your hand.

Spell title:

_____

_____

_____

Time needed:

_____

Ingredients/tools:

_____   _____

_____   _____

_____   _____

1. _____

2. _____

3. _____

4. _____

5. _____

6. _____

7. _____

Spell title:

_____

_____

_____

Time needed:

_____

Ingredients/tools:

_____   _____

_____   _____

_____   _____

1. _____

2. _____

3. _____

4. _____

5. _____

6. _____

7. _____

Spells for Health and Well-Being

In this section, you'll find health and well-being spells for focusing on the physical, spiritual, and emotional self. These spells were created to encourage personal growth and should be used in addition to—not instead of—any health plans. Use the templates that follow these spells to formulate your own health and well-being spells.

To cast these spells at their strongest, perform them on a Sunday, the day ruled by the Sun and solar deities, or Thursday, the day ruled by Jupiter. To create your own spells, you'll need to set clear intentions. Once you have a clear goal or desire in mind, you can begin collecting ingredients. To substitute or create your own spells, look to use crystals, as they have a long history of use in healing practices. Energy work can also be beneficial for blockages and energy shortages.

For the three spells included, I chose a healing runes spell, a well-being crystal grid spell, and a vitality check-in spell. The healing runes spell is a great way to get started with using runes in your practice. The well-being crystal grid spell promotes well-being with the help of a crystal grid. The third spell is a magical check-in that will allow you to use the energy of the Sun.

Healing Runes Spell

Runes are an easy introductory divination system because there are only 24 symbols to learn and they can be made by drawing the symbols on stones, shells, or even coins. Once your runes are created, you can begin your cast and interpretation. If you are unsure about reading the rune stones, write down the symbols to look up their meanings.

Time needed:
30 minutes

Ingredients/tools:
Clearing tools (incense, water, candle, or besom)
24 stones, shells, or coins
1 permanent marker

1. Cleanse your altar and collect your materials.
2. Clear your stones, shells, or coins by thoroughly removing old energies and impurities.
3. Draw on one side of each stone with a symbol of the Elder Futhark runes (see page 40).
4. Place them in a pouch or cup and hold your hand over it to charge.
5. Focus on your intentions and ask something along the lines of: "What blockages are preventing me from healing?"
6. Shake the runes and pick out three to lay faceup.
7. Take note of which runes are faceup to interpret.

Well-Being Crystal Grid Spell

Use the power of crystal healing to improve your well-being. You can use clear quartz because it's a great amplifier and pain reliever that pairs well with your intentions. This grid recommends four crystals to make a basic cross or diamond shape, but you can use more crystals if available to create a stronger, more elaborate shape. To customize this spell, use rose quartz to nurture self-love, blue lace agate to ease anxiety, sunstone to boost your mood, or fluorite for all-around healing.

Time needed:
20 minutes

Ingredients/tools:
4 clear quartz crystals
Plain surface or pre-made grid

1. Cleanse your altar and grid, if you're using one.
2. Set your intentions and begin charging your crystals.
3. Hold each crystal in your hand. Visualize its energy building and infusing with your own.
4. Place each crystal on your altar in a shape of your choice.
5. Once all crystals are in place, move your hand over them as you chant: *"Healing crystals, charge and promote better well-being as long as you're connected."*
6. Leave the crystal grid undisturbed for as long as you need.

Vitality Check-in Spell

The Sun is the ruler of vitality. That's why this spell uses energy from sun deities to assess your vitality levels and help you heal. This spell works best when performed outdoors to absorb the warming light of the sun. This spell can also be paired with healing crystals, meditation, or energy work.

Time needed:
20 to 30 minutes

Ingredients/tools:
Chair or picnic blanket
Meditation music (optional)

1. Set up an area outdoors where you can sit comfortably.
2. Clear away the area and cleanse it. If you use salt to clear, please note that salt can dehydrate plants. I recommend purification water or a broom because they are the least obtrusive.
3. Sit or lie down in a comfortable position and begin focusing on your intentions. If you'd like music, you can put it on now.
4. Focus on taking long, slow, deep breaths as you release any tension or tightness in your muscles.
5. Move your awareness to your body and focus on your state of being.
6. Spend time assessing your energy. What's causing low vitality? Where is your energy waning?
7. Take as much time as you need in this state, allowing the warmth of the sun to envelop you, restoring your energy levels.
8. Once you're ready, return to your breathing, focusing on feeling energized as you come back to awareness.

Spell title:

_____

_____

_____

Time needed:

_____

Ingredients/tools:

_____   _____

_____   _____

_____   _____

1. _____

2. _____

3. _____

4. _____

5. _____

6. _____

7. _____

Spell title:

_____

_____

_____

Time needed:

_____

Ingredients/tools:

_____   _____

_____   _____

_____   _____

1. _____

2. _____

3. _____

4. _____

5. _____

6. _____

7. _____

Spells for Strength and Protection

In this section, there are three spells for strength and protection that focus on your physical, spiritual, and emotional states. Your intentions, paired with these spells, can be applied to yourself or your loved ones. Use the templates that follow these three spells to formulate your own strength and protection spells.

To cast these spells at their strongest, perform them on a Tuesday, the day ruled by Mars and warrior deities. To create your own spells, you'll need to set clear intentions. Once you have a clear goal or desire in mind, you can begin collecting ingredients. To substitute or create your own spells, look to use black crystals such as hematite, onyx, obsidian, or smoky quartz, as they are excellent grounding and protection stones.

For the three spells included, I chose an Algiz protection home spell, a banish bad vibes spell, and a strengthening warrior spell. The first spell will imbue your home with the power of the rune Algiz. The second spell is perfect for casting out negativity through energy work. You can also add fuel to this spell by adding black salt, which is renowned for its banishing properties. The third spell allows you to work with a deity and oil to imbue yourself or an object with your intentions.

Algiz Protection Home Spell

Algiz is the Elder Futhark rune of protection. Copy the rune symbol onto the walls, doors, or windows of your home to infuse protection energy. Protection rune symbols also work well when placed on clothing labels, inside shoes, or on objects that are carried. Recharge monthly for protection. This mixture will be invisible to the naked eye.

Time needed:
10 minutes

Ingredients/tools:
1 cup water
Dash of lemon juice
Image of Algiz rune

1. Cleanse your altar and prepare your ingredients.
2. Focus on your intentions and mix together your cup of water and lemon juice.
3. Dip your fingers in the mixture and begin drawing on the walls, windows, or doors of your home.
4. Close your eyes and focus on building your energy to link the protection runes together.

Banish Bad Vibes Spell

To banish negativity, fear, or unwanted energy, use black salt, which is a powerful protectant. Sprinkle it near entryways or wherever you need a boost of protective energy. Black salt is also known for its ability to break hexes or curses that you think might be cast on an object or person. If you use peppercorns or sea salt, you will have to grind them in your mortar and pestle. You can substitute black food coloring for charcoal.

Time needed:
15 minutes

Ingredients/tools:
3 tablespoons salt
1 tablespoon charcoal
1 teaspoon black pepper
1 tablespoon incense ash
Bowl or mortar and pestle
Glass jar
Photograph of yourself (optional)

1. Cleanse your altar and prepare your ingredients.
2. Set your intentions as you begin to pour the salt, charcoal, black pepper, and incense ash into a bowl, creating "black salt."
3. Thoroughly mix and adjust the recipe to your preferences. Add more charcoal for a darker salt.
4. Pour into a glass jar to seal.
5. When you're ready, sprinkle the black salt on a photograph of your-self or across a doorway and say: *"Banishing black salt, repel and deflect harm and bad vibes from me."*

Strengthening Warrior Spell

Call upon the deities Tyr, Morrighan, or Ares/Mars for strength in this warrior spell. You can empower a charm or use an oil to anoint your forehead when facing challenges and obstacles. To represent deity, you can use a statue, candle, charm, or photo of the deity you choose.

Time needed:
20 minutes

Ingredients/tools:
Representation of deity
1 or 2 drops of carrier oil

1. Cleanse your altar and set your representation of deity in the center of your altar.
2. Sit in a comfortable position and begin focusing on your intentions.
3. Take a drop of carrier oil and anoint your forehead.
4. Focus on taking long, slow, deep breaths as you release any tension or tightness in your muscles.
5. Visualize yourself walking along a path that takes you away from yourself, as you enter the domain of your chosen deity.
6. What does it look like? Are there scents or sounds?
7. Ask your chosen deity for assistance in facing your challenges. Spend time connecting to the deity's energy and, when you're ready, thank them for their assistance.
8. Slowly return down the path as you move your awareness to your breathing.

Spell title:

_____

_____

_____

Time needed:

_____

Ingredients/tools:

_____   _____

_____   _____

_____   _____

1. _____

2. _____

3. _____

4. _____

5. _____

6. _____

7. _____

Spell title:

_____

_____

_____

Time needed:

_____

Ingredients/tools:

_____   _____

_____   _____

_____   _____

1. _____

2. _____

3. _____

4. _____

5. _____

6. _____

7. _____

Spells for the Moon Phases

In this section, you can work with the different phases of the Moon to deepen your relationship to the lunar cycle I covered in chapter 1. Use the template that follows these three spells to formulate your own strength and protection spell. You can also tap into the lunar energy by performing these spells on a Monday, the day ruled by the Moon and lunar deities.

To create your own spells, you'll need to set clear intentions. Once you have a clear goal or desire in mind, you can begin collecting ingredients. To substitute or create your own spells, you can substitute other items or tools with lunar properties.

I chose a manifestation spell for the new moon, a dream spell for the waxing moon, and a release spell for the full moon. New moons are about new beginnings and ideas, so a manifestation spell works wonders. Waxing moons center around exploration, listening to your dreams, and progress, making a dream spell an excellent way for you to begin working with the power of dreams and their meanings. Full moons are full of powerful energy that can be released or sent out into the world to carry your intentions.

New Moon Manifestation Spell

The new moon marks the beginning of the lunar cycle, offering limitless potential and new beginnings. Harness this energy by planting new ideas and goals. This is also a perfect time for working with the energy of personal improvement, manifestation, and divination. This spell can also be performed outside.

Time needed:
30 minutes

Ingredients/tools:
Representation of deity (optional)
White candle
Lighter or match
Journal
Pen

1. Cleanse your indoor or outdoor altar and tools.
2. Set your intentions for manifestation and decide if you'll be connecting with deity.
3. Light your candle and allow yourself to relax.
4. Focus on your breathing as you think about all your potential new ideas, plans, or projects. What specifically do you want to use the new moon energy to manifest?
5. Journal your responses and thoughts.
6. When you're unable to write any more, turn your attention to the Triple Goddess.
7. Ask her for guidance and write down any new instructions or thoughts.
8. Thank deity for their assistance and reflect on your time.

Waxing Moon Dream Spell

The waxing moon marks the growing phases of the moon and the Maiden aspect of the goddess. It's a time of exploration, listening to your dreams, and progress. This dream spell is performed right before bed and can be adjusted by scent. Lavender, mugwort, and valerian are excellent dream herbs to burn.

Time needed:
30 minutes

Ingredients/tools:
Incense (stick, cone, or loose on a charcoal disk)
Lighter or match

1. Cleanse your altar and light your incense.
2. Sit or lie down in a comfortable position and set your intentions.
3. Ask for the Maiden aspect of the Triple Goddess to assist with your dreams.
4. Begin long, slow, deep breaths, inhaling and exhaling as you release any tension or tightness in your muscles.
5. Move your awareness to your mind. Don't rush—allow 20 minutes of quiet.
6. Visualize silence and your thoughts clearing away, making space for dreams to thrive.
7. Return to your breathing, focusing on feeling lighter as you come back to awareness.
8. Thank deity for their assistance. Make sure your incense is no longer lit. You are now ready to sleep.

Full Moon Release Spell

The full moon is the brightest phase of the lunar cycle. It's representative of the Mother aspect of the Goddess. The energy is also strongest during this phase. You can turn this spell into a longer ritual by casting a circle of protection and preparing offerings for deity. Allow gratitude to take root and release all that's out of your control. This spell uses movement as the energy component.

Time needed:
30 minutes

Ingredients/tools:
White or silver candle
Lighter or match
Music (optional)
Crystal

1. Cleanse your indoor or outdoor altar and tools.
2. Set your intentions and light your candle. If you have music, you can put it on now.
3. Call upon the Mother aspect of the Triple Goddess to assist with energy of release.
4. Hold a crystal in your hand and connect with your energy.
5. Allow it to build and begin to move, sway, or dance.
6. Let the Goddess and energy guide your movements as you move to the rhythms of the moon.
7. With each step, release what you want to let go of in order to move forward.
8. Take your time and when you're left feeling centered and grounded, thank deity for their assistance.

Spell title:

_____

_____

_____

Time needed:

_____

Ingredients/tools:

_____   _____

_____   _____

_____   _____

1. _____

2. _____

3. _____

4. _____

5. _____

6. _____

7. _____

CHAPTER **5**

Recipes and Rituals for the Wiccan Life

I n this chapter, you'll learn all about the plants that play a major role in Wiccan life. Plants hold energy, vibrations, and power that, when harnessed, allow you to work in harmony with the Earth. We'll explore the profiles of 10 herbs and 14 essential oils and put that newfound plant knowledge into action with recipes for brewing teas and crafting herbal baths.

The Power of Plants

Working with plants is one of the many ways Wiccans connect with nature and its energy. Plants have been used to heal since long before there was written history. Archaeologists have found evidence of plants being used medicinally during the Paleolithic period, which was approximately 2.5 million years ago. Each plant holds healing and magical properties that have been used throughout history, in all parts of the world.

An herb's properties come from its origin, which is often hazy and based on myth. An example of this is rose (*Rosa* spp.), one of the most popular plants in the world. It has been used in love magic and beauty preparations for centuries. Different Greek myths relate the origin of the rose to Aphrodite, the Goddess of love and beauty. These tales stay with the plant throughout time.

The Magical Use of Herbs

Magical herbalism uses the properties found within each plant to make preparations created during spells and rituals. These creations are intended to manifest change that mirrors the practitioner's intentions. The action of combining your intention with creation harnesses magic.

An herb's origin plays a significant role in what makes it magical. In this section, I'll share 10 herbs commonly found in a Wiccan's practice. These herbs are available in most areas, and have a wide range of properties that can be used in many different preparations, spells, and rituals. There are many types of preparations you can make with herbs—oils, teas, balms, salves, incense, dressings for candles, charms, poppets, spell jars, and offerings for deity or the elements. But the preparation doesn't always have to be elaborate; sometimes, the most powerful way to use an herb is simply to burn it.

Below, you'll notice some herbs have the letters "spp." next to the botanical name. This references the entire species of that plant. This is often used when the species has hundreds of varieties and hybrids that can be used.

Basil

Botanical names: *Ocimum sanctum* or *tenuiflorum, Ocimum basilicum*

Common names: Holy basil, tulsi, sacred basil, sweet basil, St. Joseph's Wort, great basil

Family: Lamiaceae (Mint family)

Magical properties: Love, wealth, luck, flying, protection, prosperity, purification, peace

Basil is a popular culinary and aromatic herb that is found in spice racks around the world. It's versatile and used for attraction, protection, and banishing magic. It's most often used in flavoring foods, like teas, incense, and oils. Holy basil (*Ocimum sanctum*) is often found in India and Asia, while sweet basil (*Ocimum basilicum*) is found in Africa and Asia.

Chamomile

Botanical names: *Matricaria chamomilla, Chamaemelum nobile*

Common names: German chamomile, Roman chamomile, camomile, scented mayweed, ground apple

Family: Asteraceae (Sunflower family)

Magical properties: Money, healing, emotions, peace, love, tranquility, purification

Chamomile is a relaxing and aromatic herb used in many tea recipes for its calming effects. It's popular for promoting peace and tranquility in practitioners who are stressed or need sleep. It's also known for attracting love and money, and is used in purification oils, brews, and sachets prior to ritual. German chamomile (*Matricaria chamomilla*) is most often used in America, while Roman chamomile (*Chamaemelum nobile*) is used in Europe.

Cinnamon

Botanical names: *Cinnamomum cassia, Cinnamomum verum*

Common names: Cassia cinnamon, Chinese cinnamon, true cinnamon, sweet wood

Family: Lauraceae (Laurel family)

Magical properties: Success, healing, psychic powers, lust, protection

Cinnamon is an aromatic bark that is often used to flavor desserts and drinks. It's also mixed into incense, oils, and sachets. Ceylon cinnamon (*Cinnamomum verum*) is most often from Sri Lanka and Southern India, while cassia cinnamon (*Cinnamomum cassia*) is found in China. Cinnamon is often used in spell jars, teas and coffees, charms, drinks, essential oils, infused oils, and incense.

Dandelion

Botanical name: *Taraxacum officinale*

Common names: Dandelion, blowball, cankerwort, Irish daisy, monk's head, priest's crown, swine snout, wild endive, witch gowan, yellow gowan

Family: Asteraceae (Sunflower family)

Magical properties: Divination, wishes, spirit communication, psychic powers, luck

Dandelion is a hardy herb often referred to as a weed. It's found on lawns and gardens throughout the world. It's a very easy herb to use because you can use all parts of the plant in your practice. It's often used dried in incense blends, oils, and charms.

Lavender

Botanical name: *Lavandula* spp.

Common names: Elf leaf, spike

Family: Lamiaceae (Mint family)

Magical properties: Healing, love, peace, happiness, protection, longevity, purification

Lavender is an aromatic shrub native to the Mediterranean region and southern Europe, as well as parts of northern Africa, northeast India, and Southeast Asia. There are over 30 species and hybrids that are dried for tea, used to create oils, charms, and spell jars, and blended in incense for its pleasant scent.

Mint

Botanical name: *Mentha* spp.

Common names: Garden mint, peppermint, spearmint

Family: Lamiaceae (Mint family)

Magical properties: Money, lust, healing, travel, exorcism, protection

Mint is found all over the world and has over 7,000 species. It's valued for its strong aromatics and flavor. The most common mints are peppermint (*Mentha* × *piperita*) and spearmint (*Mentha spicata*). It's often used to make teas, charms, spell jars, tinctures, essential oils, and infused oils.

Mugwort

Botanical name: *Artemisia vulgaris*

Common names: Mugwort, felon herb, St. John's plant, sailor's tobacco, naughty man, chrysanthemum weed, wild wormwood

Family: Asteraceae (Sunflower family)

Magical properties: Strength, psychic powers, protection, dreams, healing, astral projection

Mugwort is considered a weed and can often be found along roadsides near highways or at the edges of parking lots—sometimes even growing right through the pavement. It has been used throughout both Europe and Asia for protection from evil spirits, disease, and bad luck. It's often used in incense and smudge sticks because of its protection properties.

Rosemary

Botanical name: *Rosemarinus officinalis*

Common names: Polar plant, compass weed, dew of the sea, garden rosemary, Mary's mantle, old man

Family: Lamiaceae (Mint family)

Magical properties: Protection, love, lust, mental powers, exorcism, purification, healing, sleep

Rosemary is a shrub native to Europe that is often used in food and to make teas, tinctures, vinegars, ritual baths, sachets, spell jars, essential oils, and infused oils.

Sage

Botanical name: *Salvia officinalis*

Common names: Garden sage, white sage

Family: Lamiaceae (Mint family)

Magical properties: Immortality, longevity, wisdom, protection, wishes

Sage is a popular metaphysical herb with over 500 species. White sage (*Salvia apiana*) is sacred in many Shamanic and Native American belief systems and is used for smudging. Sage in general has long been used to promote long life and increased wisdom. It's often used in incense, essential oils, infused oils, and charms.

Yarrow

Botanical name: *Achillea millefolium*

Common names: Achillea, carpenter's weed, death flower, devil's nettle, eerie, field hops, green arrow, soldiers' woundwort, staunch weed, wound wort, yarroway

Family: Asteraceae (Sunflower family)

Magical properties: Courage, divination, love, psychic powers, exorcism

Yarrow takes its name from the Greek hero Achilles, and is native to Europe and Asia. It's often used in charms, spell jars, infused oils, incense, and tinctures.

You probably already have many of the herbs discussed in this section. Which do you have in your home? Which can you easily acquire? These herbs will make up your own Wiccan pantry, for use in future spells and rituals.

Essential Oils

Essential oils are liquefied versions of plants that retain their magical properties. They are made by distilling plants with steam or water or by cold-pressing them, creating an easy way to incorporate them into sprays or ointments. Because of the lengthy oil-making process, as well as the amount of equipment, it's best to buy essential oils instead of blending your own.

When choosing essential oils to use in your practice, first and foremost, explore the scents. Because different scents appeal to everyone, the choice is entirely up to you and what you prefer.

You can use essential oils in a diffuser or in sprays. It is important to note that applying essential oil that hasn't been diluted with carrier oil can result in skin irritation. Carrier oils like olive, coconut, avocado, sunflower, and others are available in bulk in most supermarkets. If you intend to use oil blends on your face, look at specialty oils that aren't as greasy feeling, such as jojoba or rosehip—but be warned, the price will be a little higher than other oils.

Bergamot (*Citrus bergamia*)

Magical properties: Money, prosperity, protection, amplifying

Bergamot is a citrus oil that calms and uplifts during stressful situations. Use it in blends for wealth and power. It pairs well with citrus, spicy, woody, or florals.

Black Pepper (*Piper nigrum*)

Magical properties: Protection, courage

Black pepper is a warming oil that blends protection and courage into your magical workings. Use it in blends for its heat and protective properties. It pairs well with other spicy or woody oils.

Clary Sage (*Salvia sclarea*)

Magical properties: Dreams, divination, courage, psychic powers

Clary sage is a rejuvenating essential oil that, when used alone or added to blends, helps strengthen the mind for divination, confidence, and power. Use in skincare blends for its amplifying energy for dreams, meditation, and divination. It pairs well with citrus or florals.

Clove (*Eugenia caryophyllata*)

Magical properties: Healing, love, protection, courage, purification

Clove is a stimulating, warming, and spicy essential oil. Use it for both attracting and exorcising oil blends. It pairs well with spicy oils or florals.

Eucalyptus (*Eucalyptus radiata*)

Magical properties: Healing, purification, cleansing

Eucalyptus is a powerful purifier. Use it in sprays or oils for cleansing, healing, and cleaning. Its strong scent also encourages vitality and energy, and pairs well with mint, citrus, or florals.

Frankincense (*Boswellia carterii*)

Magical properties: Spirituality, power, purification, consecration

Frankincense is named the King of Oils and has an earthy, uplifting aroma that's perfect for grounding and spiritual connectedness. It's used in cleansing and consecrating tools, and for sprays and oils for altar work. It pairs well with most oils.

Lavender (*Lavandula angustifolia*)

Magical properties: Love, peace, protection, longevity, purification

Lavender is a calming and relaxing essential oil that promotes peace and eases feelings of anxiety or stress. It's used topically in oils, in sprays, and in incense for meditation, ritual work, or dream magic. It pairs well with most oils.

Lemon (*Citrus limon*)

Magical properties: Purification, clarity, friendship, awareness

Lemon is a cleansing, purifying, and invigorating essential oil. Use it in purification blends, alternative cleaners, and sprays for altar work or use prior to blessings. It pairs well with most oils.

Patchouli (*Pogostemon cablin*)

Magical properties: Money, lust, love, fertility

Patchouli essential oil has a grounding, sweet musk, and earthy aroma. Use it for dressing money candles and in skin blends for love, lust, or fertility. It pairs well with woody, spicy, citrus, and floral oils.

Peppermint (*Mentha piperita*)

Magical properties: Money, lust, healing, travel, exorcism, protection

Peppermint essential oil is a hybrid of water mint and spearmint and has a high menthol content. It stimulates, soothes, uplifts, and calms, making it ideal for sprays or diffusers for sleep, or blends used for the mind. It pairs well with woody, evergreen, citrus, and spicy oils.

Rose (*Rosa damascena*)

Magical properties: Healing, love, protection, emotional mind

Rose essential oil is named the Queen of Oils, and is often desired for its aroma and powerful emotional benefits. Use it in love blends and sprays. It pairs well with most oils.

Sandalwood (*Santalum album*)

Magical properties: Healing, protection, spirituality, meditation

Sandalwood essential oil has a sweet, woody aroma that is often used in diffusers or in blends for relaxing and balancing the mind. It pairs well with spicy and citrus oils.

Tea Tree (*Melaleuca alternifolia*)

Magical properties: Strength, purification, protection

Tea tree essential oil is known for its purifying and cleansing properties. Use it in sprays or a diffuser to clear the air and provide strength and protection. It pairs well with citrus, mint, evergreen, and floral oils.

Ylang ylang (*Cananga odorata*)

Magical properties: Exorcism, protection, courage, sacred

For centuries, ylang ylang essential oil has been used in ceremonies for its ability to protect, make sacred, and banish negativity. It's a calming oil that also promotes courage and confidence. Use it in sacred and protection blends and sprays. It pairs well with citrus, spicy, and woody oils.

Witchy Recipes for a Magical Brew

One way to work with herbs is through brewing magical teas or tisanes. Brewing is often incorporated into ritual or performed as a spell all on its own. By making a cup of herbal tea, you can infuse it with your intentions and the properties of the herb.

To turn tea-making into a ritual, follow these steps:

1. Cleanse and clear your space.

2. Boil your kettle or small pot of water.

3. Turn off heat and infuse 1 to 2 teaspoons of herb for 10 minutes in a mug. You can use a tea ball or place the tea directly into the cup to create an infusion. If you're using roots, add them into the small pot and simmer for 15 minutes to create a decoction. The hardy roots and woods need stronger methods to extract the flavor.

4. While it's infusing, focus on your intentions. If you like chanting or creating incantations, you can do so now.

5. Strain the tea and enjoy. To make bitter herbs more palatable, you can add honey or lemon to taste. To add caffeine, you can also add green or black tea to any mixture.

By allowing 10 to 15 minutes for setting your intentions, you're building energy and infusing it into the mug or pot. In the next section, I'll be sharing five of my favorite tea recipes for purification, rejuvenation, tranquility, psychic healing, and dreaming. Use these examples to kickstart your own tea brewing practice, then use the knowledge you've learned to create your own blends in the blank spaces after the recipes.

Lavender Rosemary Purification Iced Tea

Lavender and rosemary are two powerful protection herbs. When combined, lavender assists in making rosemary more palatable, and the duo makes for a wonderful iced tea. This recipe can also be adapted for hot tea, and you can substitute basil for rosemary if you desire.

Ingredients/tools:

Kettle

1 cup water

Tea ball or strainer

Mug

1 teaspoon dried lavender

1 teaspoon dried rosemary, or 1 rosemary sprig

4 ice cubes

Glass (optional)

Tea garnishes like lavender/rosemary or orange zest sprigs (optional)

Instructions:

1. Clear and cleanse your kitchen and prepare your ingredients.
2. Fill your kettle with the water and bring to a boil. Fill your tea ball or mug with the lavender and rosemary.
3. Pour the boiling kettle water over the herbs and infuse for 10 minutes.
4. Focus on your intentions for purification during this time.
5. Strain the tea. Add in 1 or 2 ice cubes before transferring to a glass of ice. Alternatively, you can add ice to the mug to enjoy.
6. Garnish with more lavender, rosemary, or orange zest if desired. Add honey or lemon juice to taste or enjoy alone.
7. As you drink, envision white light washing over your being, taking with it any negativity.

Mint Rejuvenation Tea

Mint is a soothing yet uplifting herb that is also calming, making it the perfect rejuvenating tea. You can use either fresh or dried mint for your preparation. To adapt this recipe, add lemongrass, lemon juice, or jasmine tea to add depth.

Ingredients/tools:

Kettle
1 cup water
Tea ball or strainer
Mug
1 teaspoon dried mint, or 5 to 6 fresh mint leaves
Honey or lemon juice (optional)
Tea garnishes like mint leaves or citrus zest (optional)

Instructions:

1. Clear and cleanse your kitchen and prepare your ingredients.
2. Fill your kettle with the water and bring to a boil. Fill your tea ball or mug with the dried or fresh mint.
3. Pour the boiling water over the herbs and infuse for 10 minutes.
4. Focus on your intentions for rejuvenation during this time. You could also pair with an incantation, such as: *"Herbal mint, soothe, restore, and rejuvenate my spiritual, emotional, and physical state."*
5. Take the tea ball out or strain. If you're using large mint leaves, you could leave these in, as they are easy to drink around. The tea will continue to steep if you do so.
6. Add honey or lemon juice to taste if desired.
7. Garnish with more mint or any citrus zest if desired.
8. As you drink, envision white light washing over you, uplifting and soothing your body.

Cinnamon Chamomile Tranquility Tea Latte

Chamomile is a peaceful herb that promotes tranquility, and cinnamon is a powerful amplifier. This recipe calls for milk to create a latte, but vegan milks such as almond or oat milk can also be used. To adapt this recipe, add other spices like nutmeg or allspice for depth.

Ingredients/tools:
1 cup milk (or vegan milk)
Small pot
2 teaspoons dried chamomile
1 teaspoon vanilla extract
Pinch of ground cinnamon
Strainer
Large mug
Tea garnishes like a cinnamon stick or ground nutmeg or allspice
 (optional)

Instructions:
1. Clear and cleanse your kitchen and prepare your ingredients.
2. Put the milk in the pot and bring to a simmer.
3. Add in the chamomile and infuse for 10 minutes, stirring frequently.
4. Focus on your intentions for tranquility. Wave your hand clockwise over the brew, chanting: *"Chamomile, imbue tranquility through and through."*
5. Mix in the vanilla and cinnamon and take off the heat.
6. Strain into a mug. You can add garnishes if you desire.
7. As you drink, repeat the chant and focus on your intentions.

Dandelion Yarrow Psychic Healing Tea

By mixing dandelion with yarrow flowers, this healing blend amplifies psychic energy. When roasted, dandelion root can taste similar to a gentle black coffee. If you're not already an avid tea drinker, this may be a great way to introduce it into your practice.

Ingredients/tools:
Small pot
1 cup water
1 teaspoon roasted dandelion root
1 teaspoon dried yarrow
Strainer
Mug
1 teaspoon vanilla extract
Tea garnishes like citrus zest or mint leaves (optional)

Instructions:
1. Clear and cleanse your kitchen and prepare your ingredients.
2. Fill the pot with the water and bring to a boil.
3. Add in the dandelion root and simmer for 15 minutes, stirring frequently.
4. Focus on your intentions for psychic healing. Wave your hand clockwise over the brew, chanting: *"Dandelion heal, dandelion amplify."*
5. Mix in the yarrow and turn off the heat, steeping for another 10 minutes.
6. Wave your hand clockwise over the brew, chanting: *"Yarrow heal, yarrow amplify."*
7. Strain into a mug. Add garnishes like citrus zest if desired.
8. As you drink, envision healing light washing over you.

Mugwort Dream Tea

Mugwort is often called the dream herb. It's a versatile plant that protects the mind and assists with dreams and astral travel. To adapt this recipe, add any citrus, mint, or florals you like.

Ingredients/tools:

Kettle
1 cup water
Tea ball or strainer
Mug
1 teaspoon dried mugwort
Honey or lemon juice
Tea garnishes like citrus zest (optional)

Instructions:

1. Clear and cleanse your kitchen and prepare your ingredients.
2. Fill your kettle with the water and bring to a boil. Fill your tea ball or mug with the mugwort.
3. Pour the boiling water over the herb and infuse for 10 minutes.
4. During this time, quietly envision your intentions and what you desire from your dreams.
5. Take the tea ball out or strain.
6. Add honey or lemon juice to taste and garnish with the citrus zest if desired.
7. As you drink, allow yourself to relax, thinking only of your intentions.

What kind of magical tea appeals to you? What purpose would it fulfill? Use the following templates to create recipes for your own magical brews.

Tea recipe:

_____

_____

_____

Ingredients/tools:

_____   _____

_____   _____

_____   _____

1. _____

2. _____

3. _____

4. _____

5. _____

6. _____

7. _____

8. _____

9. _____

Tea recipe:

_____

_____

_____

Ingredients/tools:

_____   _____

_____   _____

_____   _____

1. _____

2. _____

3. _____

4. _____

5. _____

6. _____

7. _____

8. _____

9. _____

Spiritual Baths

Herbs aren't just good for brewing tea; they can also be used for ritual baths. In Wicca, baths are multi-purpose: They can be used for cleansing and purification prior to ritual, help wash away and banish stress and negativity, and make room for new, healing energy to take root.

To prepare for a spiritual bath, follow these steps:

1. Cleanse your bathroom.

2. Set your intention.

3. Gather your ingredients.

4. Draw your bath.

5. Soak or wash, focusing on your intentions.

6. Add in chants, incantations, or energy work.

7. Drain and pack up your bath.

In addition to herbs, ritual baths might include ingredients and tools like candles; flower petals; essential oils; honey; oats; baking soda; sea, Himalayan, or Epsom salts; and goat, whole, coconut, or buttermilks. When adding salts to your bath, it's important to stay hydrated. When using herbs in the bath, make sure you have a filter fitted over the drain, so that it doesn't clog. When adding essential oils, always pre-mix them with about one tablespoon of carrier oil, so they can properly dilute.

In the next section, I provide five herbal baths for peace, self-love, stress relief, energy, and spiritual cleansing that you can try, before using the templates provided at the end of the section to craft your own.

Lavender Basil Peace Bath

This bath incorporates lavender essential oil, fresh basil, and a blue candle—all ingredients that promote peace. Bicarbonate of soda, or baking soda, assists in cleaning negativity from your aura, and leaves your skin feeling soft and smooth.

Ingredients/tools:

1 cup sea salt or Himalayan salt

¼ cup baking soda

1 cup fresh basil leaves

6 drops of lavender essential oil diluted in 1 tablespoon carrier oil, or
    1 cup lavender

Small blue votive candle (can substitute pillar or tea lights)

Instructions:

1. Cleanse your bathroom.

2. Draw your bath and add in the salt, baking soda, basil, and lavender oil blend.

3. Light the blue candle and get in the tub.

4. Soak for 15 to 20 minutes, focusing on peace and tranquility. Feel the bathwater and candle infuse your body with peace.

Rose Bath for Self-Love and -Acceptance

This bath is perfect for generating greater acceptance of your physical, mental, emotional, and spiritual self. It incorporates rose essential oil, rose petals, and rose quartz for a powerhouse of self-love energy. Epsom salt is cleansing, reduces inflammation, and assists with muscle function.

Ingredients/tools:

1 cup Epsom salt

6 drops of rose essential oil diluted in 1 tablespoon carrier oil

Handful of rose petals (optional)

Rose quartz crystal

Instructions:

1. Cleanse your bathroom.
2. Draw your bath and add in the salt and rose oil blend. Add the rose petals if desired.
3. Sit in the tub and hold the rose quartz in your dominant hand.
4. Soak for 15 to 20 minutes, focusing on the things you love about yourself. Feel the bathwater infuse your body and the rose quartz with love and acceptance.
5. Whenever you need a boost of self-love and -acceptance, hold the charged rose quartz.

Bergamot and Chamomile Stress Relief Bath

Both bergamot essential oil and chamomile flowers promote stress relief through their magical properties. Epsom salt is also a great addition for its cleansing and relaxing actions. In this bath, I recommend using blue lace agate, but other stress-reducing stones such as amethyst, clear quartz, or black tourmaline may also be used.

Ingredients/tools:

1 cup Epsom salt

6 drops of bergamot essential oil diluted in 1 tablespoon carrier oil, or
   1 cup diced fresh citrus fruits

1 cup dried chamomile flowers (optional)

Blue lace agate

Instructions:

1. Cleanse your bathroom.
2. Draw your bath and add in the salt and bergamot oil blend. Add the chamomile flowers if using.
3. Sit in the tub and hold the blue lace agate in your dominant hand.
4. Soak for 15 to 20 minutes, focusing on banishing stress. Feel the bathwater infuse your body and the agate melt away stress and anxiety.
5. Whenever you need to reduce stress, place the blue lace agate on your forehead.

Aromatic Eucalyptus and Sage Energy Bath

Eucalyptus is known for promoting vitality and energy, while sage, which pairs well with eucalyptus, is popular for its ability to amplify energy. I recommend using only a few drops of eucalyptus in this bath, as it's very potent. Feel free to add in any additional herbal flowers, if desired.

Ingredients/tools:

2 drops of eucalyptus essential oil diluted in 1 tablespoon carrier oil, or
    1 cup fresh eucalyptus leaves
10 drops clary sage essential oil diluted in 1 tablespoon carrier oil, or
    1 cup fresh sage leaves
Blue lace agate

Instructions:

1. Cleanse your bathroom.
2. Draw your bath and add in the oils.
3. Sit in the tub and hold the blue lace agate in your dominant hand.
4. Soak for 15 to 20 minutes, focusing on banishing stress. Feel the bathwater infuse your body and the agate melt away stress and anxiety.
5. Whenever you need to reduce stress, place the blue lace agate on your forehead.

Milk and Honey Spiritual Cleansing

Milk and honey are famous for their healing and cleansing properties, which is why the milk and honey bath has been a staple among witches for centuries.

Ingredients/tools:

Lighter or match

White candles (one pillar or multiple tea lights)

Jar or cup

2 cups full-fat milk or goat milk

½ cup honey

2 or 3 drops of frankincense essential oil diluted in 1 tablespoon carrier oil

Instructions:

1. Cleanse your bathroom.

2. Draw your bath and light your candles.

3. In a jar or cup, add the milk, then stir in the honey and essential oil to fully incorporate.

4. Add the milk mixture to your bath and soak for 15 to 20 minutes.

5. Focus your intentions on cleansing. Feel the bathwater infuse your body and wash away negativities and blockages.

What intentions would you like to focus on with your spiritual bath? Use the following templates to create recipes for your own spiritual baths.

Spiritual bath title:

_____

_____

_____

Ingredients/tools:

_____   _____

_____   _____

_____   _____

1. _____

2. _____

3. _____

4. _____

5. _____

6. _____

7. _____

8. _____

9. _____

Spiritual bath title:

_____

_____

_____

Ingredients/tools:

_____   _____

_____   _____

_____   _____

1. _____

2. _____

3. _____

4. _____

5. _____

6. _____

7. _____

8. _____

9. _____

CHAPTER 6

Candle Magic

By merely lighting a candle, you can invoke its properties for magic. Candles can help with manipulating energy, adding power to spells, providing visions through divination, representing the element of fire, and calling on the divine. You can also dress candles with oils and herbs, and carve them with symbols and sigils. This chapter will cover the power of fire; color correspondences for candles; how to cleanse, consecrate, and charge your candles; and how to cast spells with candle magic.

The Power of Fire

Fire warms, illuminates, and transforms. In fact, it is the element of transformation. It's associated with health, strength, and creativity, and embodies the power of the Sun—which makes it useful for the darker half of the year, when there is less warmth.

For centuries, fire has provided humans with light and heat. It's a powerful element that commands respect. Left unchecked, it can run wild, so fire safety is important to practice when performing candle magic, or any other ritual involving fire.

Candle Magic

Candles allow you to connect with the unseen energy all around you, which is why candle magic is one of the easiest ways to jump into practicing magic. When burned with intention, candles take your desires and amplify your thoughts—that's why candles are sometimes referred to as "intention messengers."

Candles are a great way to work with the elements. When used in ritual, candle colors have the ability to represent the individual elements: blue for water, green for earth, yellow for air, red for fire, and white for spirit. Another way to work with the elements is through the different parts of the candle itself. It's like a tiny elemental package: The candle flame represents fire, the melting wax can represent water, the smoke can represent air, and the wick can represent earth.

But candle magic doesn't stop with representing elements. You can also use candles to enhance your magical practice by utilizing color correspondences.

Color Correspondences

You can find candles in just about any color. But there's more to picking out a candle than just color-coordinating with your altar (though that could be fun!). Colors have their own magical properties. These color properties extend beyond candles into clothing, crystals, themes, and decor, but color correspondences are used most often with candle colors. Candles are a great way to start working with color magic—before you know it, the color correspondences will be second nature to you.

White

Deities: Aphrodite/Venus (Greek/Roman), Cerridwen (Celtic), Artemis/Diana (Greek/Roman), Selene/Luna (Greek/Roman), Triple Goddess (Wicca), Arianrhod (Celtic), Athena/Minerva (Greek/Roman), Epona (Celtic), Chloris/Flora (Greek/Roman)

Planet: Moon

Properties: Cleansing, completeness, enlightenment, healing, higher self, innocence, insight, lunar magic, meditation, peace, purification, spirit, truth

White candles can represent the Triple Goddess, or the element of spirit on a Wiccan altar. They can be used in spellwork relating to the moon, healing, and cleansing.

Black

Deities: Triple Goddess (Wicca), Hades/Pluto (Greek/Roman), Hecate/Hekate (Greek/Roman), Hera/Juno (Greek/Roman), Morrighan (Celtic), Nyx/Nox (Greek/Roman), Persephone/Proserpina (Greek/Roman), Thanos/Mors (Greek/Roman)

Planets: Saturn, Pluto

Properties: Banishing, binding, Crone aspect of the Triple Goddess, death, debts, divination, endings, exorcism, manifestation, meditation, mourning, mystery, protection, repelling energy, resurrection, sacrifice, separation, spirits, stability, structure, transformation, unconscious, uncrossing

Black candles are often labeled as bad or evil, but that isn't the case. Black candles are used for protection and to honor spirits. They're also useful for banishing magic.

Red

Deities: Aed (Celtic), Nemesis/ Invidia (Greek/Roman), Aodh (Celtic), Brighid (Celtic), Dionysus/ Bacchus (Greek/Roman), Eros/ Cupid (Greek/Roman), Hestia/ Vesta (Greek/Roman), Prometheus (Greek/Roman), Hephaestus/ Vulcan (Greek/Roman)

Planet: Mars

Properties: Energy, health, love, passion, power, protection, romance, sex, strength, vitality

Red candles are popular choices for magic related to romantic love and passion, but they can also be used for health, energy, strength, and protection. Red is a fierce color and so is the magic it creates. Red candles represent the element of fire, and can be substituted for yellow or orange to represent the Sun.

Pink

Deity: Aphrodite/Venus (Greek/ Roman)

Planet: Venus

Properties: Affection, emotions, femininity, friendship, love, peace, self-love

Pink candles are popular for their self-love properties, as well as their ability to balance emotions and inspire peace. They are ideal for all types of love.

Yellow

Deities: Demeter/Ceres (Greek/Roman), Lugh (Celtic), Helios/Sol (Greek/Roman)

Planets: Sun, Mercury

Properties: Concentration, confidence, happiness, logic, memory, mental exercises, wisdom

Yellow candles are most often used for magic relating to intellect and the mind. It is also the color that can represent the warmth of sunlight and the element of air.

Blue

Deities: Poseidon/Neptune (Greek/Roman), Lir (Celtic)

Planets: Jupiter, Neptune

Properties: Calming, confidence, harmony, health, inspiration, peace, protection, success, tranquility, truth

Blue candles are most often used in healing magic and can assist with protection against depression and anxiety. Blue candles can also represent the element of water.

Green

Deities: Arianrhod (Celtic), Demeter/Ceres (Greek/Roman), Gaia/Terra (Greek/Roman), Persephone/Proserpina (Greek/Roman), Cybele/Magna Mater (Greek/Roman), Rhea/Ops (Greek/ Roman)

Planets: Earth, Venus

Properties: Fertility, growth, healing, luck, money, prosperity

Green candles most often represent wealth, growth, and prosperity. They are also sometimes called money candles.

Purple

Deity: Athena (Greek)

Planets: Jupiter, Saturn

Properties: Astral projection, divination, dreams, memory, power, psychic abilities, psychic protection, secrets, wisdom

Purple candles represent psychic powers and mysticism. They are most often used in magic relating to psychic abilities, mental power, dreams, and memories.

Orange

Deities: Demeter/Ceres (Greek/Roman), Cronos/Saturn (Greek/Roman)

Planets: Mercury, Mars

Properties: Abundance, agriculture, confidence, creativity, energy, fertility, self-esteem

Orange candles are often associated with abundance, creativity, and agriculture. If you don't have red or yellow, orange can also be used to represent the Sun.

Brown

Deities: Gaia/Terra (Greek/Roman), Persephone/Proserpina (Greek/Roman), Cybele/Magna Mater (Greek/Roman), Joro (Norse), Sif (Norse)

Planet: Earth

Properties: Grounding, ideas, locating lost objects, protection, uncertainty

Brown candles are excellent for grounding and can assist with loss and uncertainty. They can replace green for the element of earth.

Gold

Deities: Horned God (Wicca), Tyche/ Fortuna (Greek/Roman), Lugh (Celtic), Apollo (Greek/Roman), Helios/Sol (Greek/Roman)

Planet: Sun

Properties: Recognition, wealth, worldly achievement

Gold candles can represent the Horned God. They can also substitute for any candle colors that represent fire or the Sun.

Silver

Deities: Triple Goddess (Wicca), Artemis/Diana (Greek/Roman), Selene/Luna (Greek/Roman), Hecate (Greek)

Planet: Moon

Properties: Awakening psychic abilities, divination, goals, visions

Silver candles are similar to white candles, in that they both relate to the Moon and lunar deities. In an altar setup where colored candles represent each of the five elements, you can add a silver candle to represent the Triple Goddess.

Candle Types

A candle's color isn't the only aspect that affects its magical properties. The candle's type and size also have an effect.

Candles can be made from a variety of different waxes. The waxes used indicate whether the candle has a higher burning point; a high enough burning point creates a dripless candle. While some may prefer dripless candles, you won't be able to make certain wax seals, jars, or decorations with them.

It's important to remember that the larger the candle, the longer the burn time. When beginning to work with candles, smaller ones like tea lights, votives, or chimes are best. It's important to use an unburned candle for your spells so as not to mix old energies or intentions.

Tea light

Tea lights are the smallest candle size and have a burn time of about an hour. These candles are ideal for very short spells and meditations.

Votive

Votives are the next size up and burn for about four hours. They are a great option for single-use spells, baths, and shorter rituals. They don't need a unique holder; any fire-safe plate will work.

Taper

Tapers are tall, skinny candles. They require specific holders and burn for about 12 hours. Tapers are often seen during séances and Wiccan dinner celebrations.

Chime

Chime candles are about four inches tall, look like mini-tapers, and burn for roughly three hours. Chime candles are often sold in large packs and are perfect for short, single-use spells. Like tapers, chimes need a specific holder.

Pillar

Pillars, which are the largest candle size, come in many different variations. They are often three inches wide or wider. On average, pillar candles can burn for about 30 hours. Larger pillar candles might even burn for up to 100 hours.

You can be as creative as you like when choosing your candle colors, shape, and bases. As long as you have your intentions set, you can adapt the colors accordingly to your preferences. Use this section for reference on sizes and colors to help decide which candle will best fit your needs.

Cleansing, Consecrating, and Charging Your Candles

In chapter 3, we discussed how to go about cleansing, consecrating, and charging your Wiccan tools. These methods also apply to any candles you intend to burn. Cleansing the candle is like giving it a restart and removing any old and unwanted energy. Consecration allows you to make it sacred, while charging lets you program and power it for use.

Dressing Your Candle

Dressing is an optional step that allows you to work with various oils and ground herbs for attracting and repelling energies. There are many practitioners who feel that dressing a candle is essential, while others don't dress candles at all. It's important to go with what feels right for you when performing any magic.

Choosing to dress a candle can strengthen your connection to the candle and set more powerful intentions. To dress a candle, follow these simple steps:

1. Cleanse, consecrate, and charge your candle.

2. Choose a carrier oil such as olive, grapeseed, or coconut.

3. Apply the oil to the candle with your finger, focusing on either attracting or repelling. To attract energy, start at the top of the candle and rub oil downward. To repel energy, start at the base of the candle and rub oil upward.

4. If you'd like, pick herbs that align with your intentions. Sprinkle them on the candle or roll the entire candle in a plate of ground herbs or powders.

Inscribing and Decorating Your Candle

Another optional way to work with candles is through the symbols and sigils discussed in chapter 2. You can create a brand-new sigil with your intentions or choose a rune, Ogham letter, or popular Wiccan symbol to carve into a candle before use. If you're planning on using a candle for attracting money, you'll want a money symbol, rune, or Ogham, or a sigil made from your intentions.

If you plan on both inscribing and dressing your candle, carve it before applying the oil. If you don't like working with knives or carving tools, you can create candle transfer art. To do this, you'll need a plain white pillar candle, permanent markers, plain white tissue paper, wax paper, and a hair dryer or heat gun. Follow the steps below:

1. Draw sigils or symbols on your tissue paper with your markers. Your marker will bleed through the paper, so make sure to protect the table.

2. Cut around your design so that it will fit onto the side of the candle.

3. Place your design on the spot where you'd like it to appear on your candle. Then wrap it with a piece of wax paper and hold or tape in place.

4. Heat the candle with the design pressed against it for 60 to 90 seconds. To test whether your design is sticking, peel back the wax paper. If the edges are still sticking up, press the wax paper back down and continue heating.

5. Remove the wax paper. Your design should adhere to your candle.

Alternative methods include candle varnish. The options for candle creativity are truly endless. Inscribing and decorating your candles is a great way to create spell candles with imbued intention to use or give as gifts to friends and family.

Casting Spells with Candle Magic

Candle spells are easy to perform and require only a few materials and steps. Each time you get a new candle, you'll want to cleanse, consecrate, and charge for use to get the most success out of your ritual.

To cast a candle spell:

1. Choose your candle color and size, according to your intentions.

2. Use smoke, salt, or your besom to purify and cleanse your candle. You can also technically use water, but I don't recommend it because it might damage the wick.

3. Consecrate your candle by calling upon the elements or deity, or by using an anointing oil.

4. Hold the candle in your hands and visualize, chant, or meditate your intentions.

5. Leave the candle out under the sun or full moon to charge (optional).

6. Dress, inscribe, or decorate your candle, adding power and layering your intentions.

7. If you feel called to, cast a circle before lighting your candle.

8. Perform your spell. This may consist of meditation, visualization, energy work, chanting, dancing, wax divination, scrying, or burning paper or herbs.

9. Dispose of your candle. You can do this by throwing the candle in the trash, burying it, or melting it down. If you plan on burying your candle, make sure it's made from natural materials such as beeswax and not dressed with anything that can harm the environment. If you melt down the candle, it can be poured into a mold to create a charm. This is an ideal option for spells where you want the energy to remain, such as attracting magic.

Candle spells are easy to make your own because they can be paired with any form of magic, spell, or ritual. Many witches even sell their own spell candles. If you plan on purchasing pre-made spell candles, make sure they come from a reputable shop because the shop owners will be the ones cleansing, consecrating, charging, dressing, and decorating. These candles will arrive with their intentions set, so make sure to buy ones with intentions that closely mirror what you desire.

Candle Magic Spells

In this section, you'll find four candle spells to try, each designed to inspire your own unique candle spells. The times needed to complete these spells will vary depending on your personal preferences and which types of candles are used. To create your own candle spells, remember to begin by choosing a color and size that will serve you best.

Aphrodite Love Candle Spell

Pay tribute to and ask for assistance from Aphrodite, the Greek Goddess of love and beauty, while also inspiring feelings of love. Use a pink candle for self-love or a red one for passionate love. If you don't have one of the rose ingredients, use more of one of the others.

Ingredients/tools:

1 ounce carrier oil
2 drops of rose essential oil
Small bowl
Red or pink votive candle
Plate or candle holder
4 to 5 dried rose petals
Lighter or match

1. Cleanse, consecrate, and charge your ingredients.
2. Combine the carrier oil and essential oil in a small bowl. As you do this, focus on your intentions.
3. Place your candle on a plate or holder and anoint it. With your finger, rub the oil blend starting at the top and working your way down to the base to direct your energy to attract.
4. Lightly crush the rose petals and sprinkle over your candle. If you'd like, you can keep some dried rose petals to sprinkle during the spell.
5. Light the candle, close your eyes, and allow yourself to relax. Focus on your intentions and, say: *"Goddess Aphrodite, I call upon you by candlelight, wrap me in your sensual warmth, loving energy, and healing light."*
6. Meditate, work on energy, or end your spell by extinguishing your candle and disposing of it.

Dream Drawing Candle Spell

Enhance your dreams for divination or to allow messages to become clearer. This candle spell uses mugwort, a dream-enhancing herb, as well as a purple candle for psychic enhancement. This spell is best performed prior to sleep, when the energy is strongest.

Ingredients/tools:
Purple chime or votive candle
Plate or candle holder
1 ounce dried mugwort
Lighter or match

1. Cleanse, consecrate, and charge your ingredients.
2. Place your candle on a plate or holder and surround it in a circle of dried mugwort. If you'd like, you can keep some dried mugwort to sprinkle during the spell.
3. Light the candle, close your eyes, and allow yourself to relax. Focus on your intentions and allow yourself to envision white or purple light wrapping your body in your intentions.
4. Meditate for 10 to 15 minutes, visualizing yourself unlocking a door to your dreams.
5. When you are ready, end your spell by extinguishing your candle and disposing of your candle and herbs.

Fehu Money Candle Spell

Work with the runic symbol Fehu to attract wealth and prosperity through this money candle spell. You can carve, draw, or create candle transfer art (see page 140). If you're using candle transfer art, you'll want to use a white candle. This candle spell uses a larger pillar candle, so you can repeat the same spell multiple times, or craft money charms with the wax if you desire.

Ingredients/tools:
Knife for carving or drawing tools
Image of Fehu rune
Green or white pillar candle
Lighter or match
Candle holder

1. Cleanse, consecrate, and charge your ingredients.
2. Draw the Fehu rune on your candle via your preferred method.
3. Hold the candle and charge the rune with your intentions.
4. Light the candle, place it on a plate or holder, and close your eyes and allow yourself to relax. Focus on your intentions and, say: "*Fehu, rune of wealth and prosperity. Guide me and lend me sight of money clarity.*"
5. Visualize a green or white light surrounding the candle and enveloping your being.
6. To end your spell, extinguish your candle and dispose of it. Repeat the spell as often as you'd like with your large pillar candle.

Negativity Banishment Candle Spell

Sometimes, negative energy comes your way. It's important to know how to protect yourself by banishing unwanted energy. This spell also works to break ill intentions that are directed at you.

Ingredients/tools:

1 ounce carrier oil

2 drops of ylang ylang oil

Small bowl

Black votive or chime candle

Plate or candle holder

1 ounce dried basil

Lighter or match

1. Cleanse, consecrate, and charge your ingredients.
2. Combine the carrier oil and essential oil in a small bowl. As you do this, focus on your intentions.
3. Place your candle on a plate or holder and anoint it. With your finger, rub the oil blend, starting at the bottom and working your way up the candle to direct your energy to repel.
4. Sprinkle the candle with the dried basil. If you like, you can keep some basil to sprinkle on during the spell.
5. Light the candle, close your eyes, and allow yourself to relax. Focus on your intentions and visualize the negative energy looming around you. See the candle burning away every last drop.
6. When you feel lighter and like the action has been completed, end your spell by extinguishing your candle and disposing of it.

What kind of spells do you want to create with candle magic? What intentions do you want to support? Use the following templates to create your own candle spells.

Spell title:

_____

_____

_____

Ingredients/tools:

_____   _____

_____   _____

_____   _____

1. _____

2. _____

3. _____

4. _____

5. _____

6. _____

7. _____

8. _____

9. _____

Spell title:

_____

_____

_____

Ingredients/tools:

_____   _____

_____   _____

_____   _____

1. _____

2. _____

3. _____

4. _____

5. _____

6. _____

7. _____

Spell title:

_____

_____

_____

Ingredients/tools:

_____   _____

_____   _____

_____   _____

1. _____

2. _____

3. _____

4. _____

5. _____

6. _____

7. _____

Conclusion

In each chapter of this book, we learned about formulating and creating your own rituals, spells, and recipes while also setting the traditions and principles you choose to follow and include in your journey as a Wiccan.

You're now ready to craft your own Book of Shadows with the knowledge you have gained. It's my hope that you are ready to walk the Wiccan path with confidence and develop a practice that's meaningful to you.

By beginning your own Book of Shadows, you can continue enhancing your practice. Was there one area of practice that called to you more than another? Listen to what appeals to you and dive into the areas that interest you. No matter what you feel pulled toward, there are countless books on herbs, oils, candles, deities, elements, rituals, spells, and correspondences that you can read next.

And always remember: Each practitioner follows their own values and ethics and sets their own rules. Every Book of Shadows is in its own way valid to the practitioner. What's important is your dedication and respect for yourself and your craft.

Whenever you need inspiration or assistance, flip back through and read over your prompts that you've completed. In those lines, you've started your practice and have shown dedication toward your craft. Continue forward in your journey, personalizing it, and making it your own.

Merry part and merry meet again,
Ambrosia Hawthorn

Glossary

altar: A special, flat surface for rituals or other magical workings

athame: A consecrated ritual blade used to direct energy, not to cut. Usually double-edged, with a black handle. It can be used interchangeably with a wand during casting and opening a circle of protection.

banish: To end or get rid of negative energy or unwanted spirits

bell: Often used as a ritual tool to raise energy

besom: A broom that is used to sweep energy and can cleanse or purify a space

Blue Moon: When there are two full moons in one calendar month, the second is referred to as a Blue Moon

Book of Shadows: A witch's book of spells, rituals, and magical lore

call: Invoking energy

calling the quarters: Verbal or symbolic acknowledgment of the elements in a ritual environment

cauldron: Used to house ingredients for ritual workings. Fire-safe cauldrons can be used to hold fire rituals.

chalice: A ritual cup or goblet used to hold the ale in cake and ale ceremonies or other ritual beverages

chants: Phrases or words repeated during spells or ritual to raise energy

charging: To infuse an object with energy for use

charms: An item that has been created for a specific use. They can be sachet bags, spell jars, amulets, talismans, or knots.

circle: Sacred space that is created with energy to hold rituals

cleansing: Removing negative energy from an object or space

correspondence: An item that has a magical property

craft: The practice of witchcraft

Crone: Aspect of the Goddess represented by the old woman and darker part of the year

cross-quarters: The Sabbats in between the solstices and equinoxes

dedication: The ritual or rite that an individual chooses to perform, making an oath to accept and respect their path as Wiccan or witch

divination: The act of connecting to the inner self and the universe to seek answers. Includes scrying, dowsing, tarot or oracle decks, runes, and Ogham staves.

elements: The physical elements of earth, air, fire, and water are the building blocks of the universe. The fifth element of spirit exists in all the physical elements and in divinity.

Esbat: A circle or ritual to honor the full moon. It's often used to celebrate the Goddess aspect of divinity.

Gardnerian Wicca: A tradition of witchcraft created from the teachings of Gerald Gardner

God: Masculine aspect of deity

Goddess: Feminine aspect of deity

grounding: To disperse excess energy generated during ritual by sending it into the Earth

herbalism: The art of using herbs

High Priest/ess: A coven leader who has received a certain level of initiation in their coven

Horned God: One of the most prevalent God-images in paganism. Not associated with the Christian devil or satanism.

incantation: Words spoken during ritual or spells

incense: Burning of herbs, oils, or other aromatic items to scent the air during acts of ritual. Also can be used to cleanse and purify a space.

initiation: A process where an individual is accepted or admitted into a coven. Not to be confused with dedication.

invocation: To bring or call something to you

libation: Ritually giving a portion of food or drink to a deity or spirit. Often called an "offering" or "cake and ale offering."

magic: The projection of natural energy or power to bring about change

Maiden: Aspect of the Goddess representing a young woman or girl who has not yet awakened

meditation: A quiet time, reflection, or contemplation to turning inward toward the self or divinity

Mother: Aspect of the Goddess representing motherhood, mid-life, and fertility

New Age: The mixing of newer spiritual practices with religion

occult: Meaning "hidden." Is broadly applied to a wide range of metaphysical topics that aren't often understood by the mainstream public.

Ogham: The ancient alphabet of the Celtic people. Often carved into wood to create Ogham staves, which are an equivalent to rune stones.

Old Religion: A name for paganism, as it pre-dates Christianity. Also referred to as the Old Ways.

oracle: A divination deck that connects the user with the subconscious and the universe

pagan/neo-pagan: General term for followers of Wicca and any other magical, shamanistic, or polytheistic, Earth-based religion

pantheon: A collection or group of Gods and Goddesses in a particular religious structure. Examples are Celtic, Roman, Greek, and Scandinavian.

pentacle: A circle with a five-pointed, upright star, often worn as a symbol of a witch's beliefs. It can also be used to represent the element of earth in ritual.

quarters: The north, east, south, and west parts of a circle or ritual area. Home of the physical elements.

Rede: The basic tenet of Wicca, summarized by: *"An it harm none, do what ye will."*

ritual: A ceremony or rite to honor divinity and raise and use energy for an intended purpose or celebration

ritual tools: Objects that are used in ritual and placed on an altar. Often include deity and elemental representations.

runes: A set of symbols or letters used for divination. Examples are Scandinavian, Norse, and Germanic.

Sabbat: A sun celebration including a solstice, equinox, or cross-quarter day

scrying: A method of divination. To gaze at or into an object to receive images or messages.

solitary: A pagan who often works alone and isn't a part of a coven

spell: A magical use or manipulation of energy to create an intended outcome. Often includes charms, sachets, herbalism, and incantations or chants.

Summerland: The pagan afterlife

tarot: A 78-card divination deck that connects the user with the subconscious and the universe, using specific symbolism and card meanings

tradition: A branch of paganism, often in the form of covens or groups that follow a specific path

Triple Goddess: A Goddess in all of her three aspects: Maiden, Mother, and Crone

visualization: The process of forming mental images to raise and use energy for an intended purpose

wand: A ritual tool used to direct energy. Can be used interchangeably with an athame.

Wheel of the Year: One full cycle of the seasonal year. Includes the eight Wiccan Sabbats.

Wicca: A modern pagan religion with spiritual roots

Wiccan: A practitioner of faith, particularly one that uses ritual, nature, the elements, and a reverence for the divine

witch: A practitioner of magic, particularly one that manifests change through tools and spells

witchcraft: The craft of the witch. Often including stones, colors, herbs, energy, and incantations.

Resources and Recommended Reading

The Complete Book of Incense, Oils and Brews
by Scott Cunningham

This is one of my personal favorites. After learning the basics about how herbs, spices, and plants can be used in your practice, this book will take your craft a step further and assist you in creating custom incense blends, magical oils, potions, and other useful brews.

Cunningham's Encyclopedia of Magical Herbs
by Scott Cunningham

This is a must for any beginning student of Wicca. It contains the properties, history, and uses for over 400 herbs. Use this encyclopedia whenever you need to incorporate herbs in your spells.

Seasons of Wicca: The Essential Guide to Rituals and Rites to Enhance Your Spiritual Journey by Ambrosia Hawthorn

A book that offers practical guidance and empowering rites and rituals that will bring the magic of Wicca into your daily life. Explore in-depth primers on the Wheel of the Year and the crucial purposes of the elements, then embark on your own spiritual path with step-by-step instructions for Sun Celebrations, Moon Celebrations, and Wiccan Rites.

The Spell Book for New Witches: Essential Spells to Change Your Life by Ambrosia Hawthorn

A spell book that shows you how to tap into your inner power and make spellcasting practical for your day-to-day. Find easy-to-follow spells that will help you find lasting love, protect your family and friends, advance your career, and live the life you deserve.

Wicca Crystal Magic: A Beginner's Guide to Practicing Wiccan Crystal Magic, with Simple Crystal Spells by Lisa Chamberlain

This book provides a solid foundation from which to build your own practice of working with crystals. It's a wonderful resource for working with stones, the natural teachers from deep inside the Earth, to aid you on your path no matter where it leads you.

Wicca Herbal Magic: A Beginner's Guide to Practicing Wiccan Herbal Magic, with Simple Herb Spells by Lisa Chamberlain

By the end of this guide, you'll have a solid foundation from which to build your own practice of working with 13 magical herbs. Whether you're well-practiced in other forms of magic but are just discovering herbs, or new to magic altogether, *Herbal Magic* provides an excellent place to begin your magical journey.

Witchology Magazine

A monthly magazine for modern paganism and magic. This is a valuable resource and a way to learn from a team of seasoned writers who share their own paths with their readers.

Index

A

abundance and prosperity spells, 79–82
Abundance jar spell, 80
Achilles, 109
Aed (Celtic god). *See* Gods
Ætt, 40
Áine (Celtic goddess), 26. *See also* Goddesses
air, element of, 14, 60
Aker (Egyptian god), 25. *See also* Gods
Alder moon (Celtic), 37
Algiz protection home spell, 92
altars. *See also* rituals; spells
   building of, 68–69
   cleansing of, 69
   color correspondences and, 133–137
   definition of, 152
   symbols and, 46–47
Amaunet (Egyptian goddess), 25. *See also* Goddesses
Amun (Egyptian god), 25. *See also* Gods
animism, 9
Anu (Celtic goddess), 26. *See also* Goddesses
Anubis (Egyptian god/goddess), 25. *See also* Goddesses; Gods
Anuket (Egypt goddess). *See* Goddesses
Aphrodite love candle spell, 143
Aphrodite/Venus (Greek/Roman goddess), 25. *See also* Goddesses
Apollo (Greek/Roman god). *See* Gods
"Ardanes," 4
Ares/Mars (Greek/Roman god), 25. *See also* Gods
Arianrhod (Celtic goddess), 26. *See also* Goddesses
Aromatic eucalyptus and sage energy bath, 126

Artemis/Diana (Greek/Roman goddess), 25. *See also* Goddesses
Ash moon (Celtic), 36
asteroid goddesses, 19, 21
astrological calendar, 30
astrological signs, 14, 15, 16, 17–18
athames, 14, 59, 62, 64, 68, 152
atheism, 10
Athena/Minerva (Greek/Roman goddess), 25. *See also* Goddesses
Aura (Greek/Roman goddess). *See* Goddesses
autumn equinox, 30, 34

B

Baldur (Norse god), 27. *See also* Gods
Banish bad vibes spell, 91, 93
banishing
   bells for, 62
   candle magic for, 146
   color correspondences and, 133–134
   definition of, 152
   essential oils and, 113
   herbalism and, 105
   ritual baths and, 122, 125, 126
   spells for, 91, 93
   strength and protection spells for, 91, 93
basil, 105
Bast (Egyptian goddess), 25. *See also* Goddesses
Beaver moon (Native American), 39
Belenos (Celtic god), 26. *See also* Gods
bells, 62, 152
Beltane Sabbat, 18, 22, 23, 31, 32–33
bergamot, 110
Bergamot and chamomile stress relief bath, 125
besoms, 62–63, 67, 68, 69, 141, 152

Birch moon (Celtic), 36
black pepper, 110
Blessing moon, 38
Blodeuwedd (Celtic goddess),
26. *See also* Goddesses
Blood moon, 38–39
Blue moon, 36, 39, 152
Boann (Celtic goddess), 26.
See also Goddesses
Book of Shadows, 5, 40, 46, 68, 151, 152
Book of the Law, The (Crowley), 4
Borrum (Celtic god). *See* Gods
Bowls, 62. *See also* cauldrons
Brân (Celtic god), 26. *See also* Gods
Brân (Welsh god). *See* Gods
brewing, 114–119
Brighid (Celtic goddess), 26.
See also Goddesses
broom, 62

C

Cailleach (Celtic goddess), 26.
See also Goddesses
calling the quarters, 59–60, 152
calls, 59–60, 67–68, 94, 100, 143, 152, 153
candles, 63, 131
altars and, 68
color correspondences for, 133–137
dressing, 139
element of fire and, 132
inscribing and decorating, 140
spells using, 131, 141–146
types of, 137–138
Cardea (Greek/Roman goddess).
See Goddesses
cardinal directions, 14
cauldrons, 15, 62, 63, 64, 68, 81, 152
Celtic pantheon, 26, 63
Celtic tree calendar, 30
censers, 63
centering, 56–57, 58
Cernunnos (Celtic Horned god),
24, 26. *See also* Gods

Cerridwen (Celtic goddess), 26,
63. *See also* Goddesses
chalices, 15, 63, 64, 68, 152
chamomile, 105
chants. *See also* incantations
candle magic and, 141, 143
for clearing, consecrating, and
charging tools, 67, 68
definition of, 152
ritual baths and, 122
spells and, 87
teas/tisanes and, 114, 116, 117, 118
charging
candles, 139, 141, 142, 145
definition of, 152
in health and well-being spells, 86, 87
moon phases and, 18
in prosperity and abundance
spells, 80, 82
relationship spells and, 74, 75
ritual tools, 67–68, 139
charms
candle magic and, 141, 145
definition of, 152
layered, 79, 80
sigils and, 82
spells and, 73, 74, 79, 80, 94
Chaste moon, 36
chime, 138
Chloris/Flora (Greek/Roman goddess),
25. *See also* Goddesses
cinnamon, 106
Cinnamon chamomile tranquility
tea latte, 117
circle, casting, 59–60, 62,
63–64, 71, 141, 152
clary sage, 111
cleansing. *See also* spells
altars, 69
besoms and, 62–63, 69
candles and, 133, 139,
141–142, 143–146
cleansing
color correspondences, 133–137

Acknowledgments

My thanks go to my amazing support team who helped me write this book: my wonderful husband, Leon, thank you for your encouragement during the writing process; my adorable familiar Nala, who sat with me every day while writing this book; my amazing sister Sylvia, who always pushes me to be the best that I can; and the *Witchology* team for continuing to create amazing work for the magazine while I was writing this book. Lastly, thanks to Kelly Koester, my editor, for her wonderful skills in helping the words in this book come alive.

About the Author

Ambrosia Hawthorn is a traveling eclectic pagan, astrologer, and card slinger with indigenous roots in Yup'ik shamanism and Puerto Rican folk magic. She is the founder of Wild Goddess Magick, a witchcraft blog, and the editor of *Witchology Magazine*. She discovered her practice at the age of 13, and has been studying the craft and her lineage ever since. Ambrosia's goal is to provide material for every kind of pagan, and she uses the Wheel of the Year to create and share new content about all types of magic.

CPSIA information can be obtained
at www.ICGtesting.com
Printed in the USA
JSHW051954190121
11056JS00001B/1